SURVIVING THE MAN OF GOD

SURVIVING THE MAN OF GOD

MICHAEL OGLESBY, SR.

Michael Oglesby, Sr.
Surviving "The Man of God"

Published by Spines
ISBN: 979-8-89569-277-6

Spines

CONTENTS

INTRODUCTION

SURVIVING THE MAN OF GOD

My purpose in writing this book is not to persuade readers to feel the same way I do about the House of Prayer and its late leader, Arthur Allen Jr. Instead, I aim to share my personal experiences within the organization, truthfully and transparently, so that readers can draw their own conclusions about whether this was a true Man of God or a false prophet.

This is not just my story. It's a voice for those still trapped in silence, for those who are afraid to speak out, and for those who may one day find the courage to tell their truth. I write for them.

The phrase "life, liberty, and the pursuit of happiness," enshrined in the U.S. Constitution, promises every person the right to seek joy and fulfillment. But what happens when trauma robs you of that pursuit? Abuse, neglect, and violence. These experiences can leave lasting scars. In my case, being raised in a cult shaped every corner of my life.

To illustrate this, I think of Doyle Brunson, one of the greatest poker players of all time. He won two World Series of Poker championships with the worst possible starting hand—10/2 offsuit. Life had dealt him a losing hand, but through skill, courage, and a little luck, he turned it into victory. That metaphor speaks to me deeply.

I, too, was dealt a difficult hand. But with faith in God, love for my twelve children, and the strength to endure, I survived. This is my story—Michael Oglesby Sr.—of how I rose above the trauma, the betrayal, and the pain to reclaim my life, and how I survived the man of God.

PART I
ORIGINS AND INNOCENCE

CHAPTER 1
MY EARLIEST MEMORY

BIRTHDAY JOY BEFORE THE STORM

My Worst Nightmare

It was the summer of 2011. My wife of eighteen years—the mother of our twelve children—had filed for divorce and obtained a restraining order that forced me out of our home. After thirty days, the order was dismissed by a judge, who also granted me weekend visitation rights with my children: every other Friday at 6:00 p.m. until Sunday at 6:00 p.m.

We had been together for nearly two decades, and I was eager to see my kids. That weekend, I arrived at the house full of hope. But what greeted me at the door was something I could never have imagined.

My wife opened the door on all fours, barking like a

dog. Between barks, she shouted, “Come on in, trashy-ass nigger! Hey, Pussy Lips!” As I entered, she kept calling me names—“Trashy-ass nigger,” “Pussy Lips,” and “Low-life dog.” Then she had my kids join in.

My five-year-old daughter said, “Hey, Pussy Lips!” I’m still haunted by the sound of her sweet, innocent voice saying those heinous words. My fifteen-year-old daughter followed with, “Hey, old trashy-ass nigger!” One by one, all my children—except my oldest son—surrounded me, chanting insults like “Nigger,” “Pussy Lips,” and “Low-down dirty dog,” while my wife continued barking, as if to show them what I supposedly was.

I felt like I was trapped in a horror movie—my wife and children cast as demons or zombies on the attack. Then my wife called my ten-year-old son from the back. He strutted into the room as if stepping into a boxing ring, ready for a championship fight. With a smirk, she asked him, “What did you want to ask your dad?”

My son boldly asked, “Did you eat any shit?” Another child chimed in, “Yeah, shit eater, did you eat any shit?” My wife burst out laughing between barks, cheering them on in a twisted celebration—pleased at how well they followed her orders to humiliate their father.

How It All Started

After enduring all I could, I fled the house, climbed into my vehicle, and broke down in bitter tears. It felt like I was trapped in a nightmare—one I desperately wanted to wake up from. The surreal nature of what had just happened was almost too much to process.

How could this be the outcome of more than thirty years of faithful service to the House of Prayer under Pastor Arthur Allen Jr.? How could this be the result of nearly two decades of devotion as a husband and father?

Even now, I still hear my children's voices echoing in my mind—innocent voices turned into weapons of emotional destruction. Their words tore through my spirit like bullets through flesh. The pain wasn't just in what they said—it was in knowing that their purity had been manipulated, their love turned against me.

This was the cost of leaving the "Man of God's" cult. I was demonized, ostracized, and disrespected in ways I never imagined possible—even by my own children. The experience left me shattered, but it also marked the beginning of a deeper truth: the truth of what I had survived, and the strength I would need to reclaim my life.

The Beginning of Her Wounds

My earliest memory is from my fourth birthday. I remember sitting in a chair, eating a grape popsicle, surrounded by smiling faces wishing me a happy birthday. The atmosphere was joyful—pure happiness. My cousin Adrian and I share the same birthday, though she's three years older. Our mothers, who are sisters, collaborated to throw us a joint celebration. That day was the last time I saw my cousin or my aunt for many years. Shortly after, my mother was introduced to the "Man of God."

Her father—my grandfather—was an ambitious man who owned two successful gyms in Louisiana during the 1970s. He trained clients of all backgrounds and built a reputation as a personal trainer and weightlifter, earning the nickname "Muscle Man." My grandmother managed the books and was a nurturing, attentive mother. She and my mother shared a particularly close bond.

But their success didn't last. Racial tensions in the South escalated, and white supremacists targeted my grandfather's businesses because of his interracial clientele. Acts of vandalism, threats, and slander eventually forced him to close both gyms. The family fell into financial hardship, and the trauma of that collapse rippled through their lives.

According to family accounts, things became so

desperate that my grandmother and her sister resorted to selling their bodies to survive. At that time, my grandmother only drank socially, but the weight of these experiences led her down the path of alcoholism. The family hit rock bottom and relocated to Atlanta, settling in the Summerhill neighborhood.

The marriage between my grandparents unraveled. My grandfather's infidelity and my grandmother's drinking drove them apart. In a heartbreaking decision, my grandmother walked away from the family, leaving her four children—including a newborn—with my grandfather. My mother was just two years old.

The abandonment wounded her deeply. She was so devastated that she wandered out of the house, searching the neighborhood for her mother. A group of white strangers found her at a grocery store and helped return her home. That moment marked the beginning of a lifetime of emotional scars—scars that would shape her into a rebellious child and eventually lead her into the hands of a man who claimed to be sent by God.

Being raised solely by her father added even more trauma to her young life. My grandfather was a deeply religious man and a deacon in the church. He was strict and authoritative, and he ran a very tight ship when it came to my mother and her siblings, but my mother did not make his job easy. She missed her mother so badly and would constantly run away from home with my grandfather, and would go and live with my grandmother. My grandmother at this point was an alcoholic and did not have many rules in her home for my mother to follow. Whenever my mother was living with my grandmother, she could do as she pleased. Mother would leave the house at late hours in the evening at a very early age, with no supervision. At the age of 11 years old, mother was walking down a dark street one night, and a man grabbed her from behind. It seemed as if this man had been stalking my mother, and he hid behind a wall and waited for her to pass by. As she walked past, he jumped from behind the wall and grabbed her. My mother began to scream, and the man covered her mouth. She continued to kick and tried to break away from the man, but he overpowered her and dragged her down a dark alley. She was terrified as the man violently snatched her skirt up and ripped her panties off. She kicked and struggled as much as her little body would allow her to as he forced himself inside of her tiny womb, leaving her torn and bloody. Mother did not know if the man was going to kill her or not as he was raping her. When he finished, he just left her lying on the ground and walked away. When mother talks about this tragic event, you can see and feel the fear that she felt that day, as a little girl even to this day in her voice, in her eyes, through her tears. Mother never received any kind of justice, resolution, or even counseling for this tragic violation of her innocence and she continued down the path of self-destructive behavior.

By the time mother was twelve years old, she was having a full-blown sexual affair with a grown man 24 years old. Although mother did not realize it at the time, she was still being raped even though it was consensual. My grandfather heard of my mother's promiscuousness, and he tried to intervene. Mother liked to go to grandmother's house because there were no rules that prevented her from frolicking with her 24-year-old boyfriend. He would pull up to grandmother's house in his car, and my mother would go out to the car, get in with him, and he would take advantage of her in the car. My grandfather drove to my grandmother's house one night and caught my mother in the car with the man. Grandfather snatched her out of the car and ran the man away. Grandfather then took mother away from grandmother's house and took her back to his house. Grandfather then demanded that my mother take off her clothes. He then made her lie on the bed and spread her legs, and he began to stick his fingers inside of my mother's vagina. According to him, he was checking to see if she was a virgin or not. Allegedly He also performed this same vagina check test on some of my mother's sisters as well. Mother wasn't safe at grandmother's house and now not even at grandfather's house! It's hard to say which was worse. After being molested by her father, mother left home for good.

At just fourteen, she was out on her own—making choices far beyond her years. She met a young man that she really liked, and he began to court her. She was mesmerized by this young man, and he convinced her to go to his home with her so they could spend some time together alone. My mother agreed to go with him to his house thinking that they would be alone. Once she arrived, she was surprised to find that the man had several of his male friends at the house. He took my mother to a room in the house and had sex with her. When they finished, my mother thought that the man was going to take her back home, but he told her, no, before you leave, you must have sex with all my boys. My mother said, No! I came here for you! I like you! I didn't come here to have sex with your friends! The man said, "well bitch, you are not leaving here until you let all of my boys fuck you!" My mother tried to run but the man grabbed her and pushed her into the room where all his friends were, and they all took turns raping my mother. My mother received a harsh introduction to how cold, callous, and beguiling some niggers can be. I use the word nigger, not because of the color of their skin, but it is because of how dirty and lowdown they are in character.

Each of these traumas—the loss of her mother, the abuse, the betrayal—pushed her further down a path that would ultimately lead her to the "Man of God," Arthur Allen Jr.

CHAPTER 2
MY MOTHER'S WOUNDS

A LOVE THAT WASN'T MEANT TO HEAL

At fifteen years old, my mother met my father. He was twenty-three, fresh out of the Air Force, and immediately captivated by her beauty and maturity. She looked older than her age, and he pursued her with confidence. The attraction was mutual, and they soon entered into a relationship.

Coincidentally, my father's mother and my mother's aunt were close friends and coworkers. When they discovered the relationship, they voiced their disapproval—strongly. Family members on both sides warned my father that he was too old to be involved with a fifteen-year-old girl. But neither he nor my mother listened. They continued their relationship, unaware of the storm that lay ahead.

What my mother didn't know was that my father was

battling a severe drug addiction. At sixteen, my mother became pregnant with my oldest brother. By nineteen, she was pregnant with me. At twenty-one, she had her third child—my sister. All three children were fathered by a man who drifted in and out of her life, and in and out of prison, consumed by petty crimes and addiction.

My father was a brilliant man. A straight-A student in high school, he was so intelligent that the Air Force tried to recruit him during his junior year. He initially declined, but when the Army drafted him during the Vietnam War, he returned to the Air Force recruiter for help. The recruiter ensured he would be placed in the Air Force, where he served for four years, stationed in Thailand. He worked in aircraft logistics and rose to the rank of Sergeant.

What happened during his service remains unclear, but when he returned home, he was a changed man—addicted to drugs and emotionally unstable. He married his high school sweetheart, Elizabeth, and for a time, it seemed they had built a beautiful life together: a home, two cars, good jobs, and a promising future. But one day, he came home to a "Dear John" letter. Elizabeth had left him—for her girlfriend. She confessed that she was in love with another woman and had chosen to live her truth.

The heartbreak sent my father into a downward spiral. The confusion and betrayal were overwhelming, and his addiction worsened. By the time he met my mother, he was already deeply lost in that addiction. Despite her youth and vulnerability, she became entangled in his chaos.

She had three children with him—each time hoping for stability but receiving heartbreak instead. He was in and out of prison, while she was left to raise her children alone. With only an eighth-grade education and no clear career path, my mother turned to government assistance—welfare, food stamps, and public housing. We ended up in "the projects," a place that became both our shelter and our struggle.

My mother had been dealt a difficult hand from the very beginning. Yet, she kept going. She refused to give up, even when life offered her little more than pain.

This chapter of her life wasn't just about heartbreak—it was about survival.

Grace in the Projects

My mother, older brother, younger sister, and I lived in one of Atlanta's most notorious housing projects, Perry Homes. It was a place steeped in poverty, violence, and despair. Drug dealing, addiction, prostitution, and gunfire were part of the daily soundtrack. It wasn't uncommon to step outside and see a lifeless body in the yard, another casualty of a deal gone wrong. Perry Homes felt less like a neighborhood and more like a war zone in a forgotten corner of the world.

The projects were filled with single mothers like mine, raising children alone after being abandoned by the men who had once promised love and stability. We were left to navigate life's cruelty without protection, provision, or affirmation. The absence of a father figure didn't just leave a void; it altered the trajectory of our lives.

And yet, in the midst of this chaos, my mother was a quiet force of excellence. She was a woman of remarkable talent. Everything she touched seemed to carry a sense of perfection. When she made a bed, it looked like it belonged in a showroom. When she ironed a shirt, it was crisp and flawless. Her Christmas gifts were wrapped with such precision and elegance that they could have been featured in a magazine. She cut wrapping paper with straight, clean lines—no excess, no wrinkles, just beauty. I'd look at her creations and then glance at my own clumsy attempts, which resembled something a kindergartener might produce.

One day, while watching a documentary about Martha Stewart, I found myself thinking of my mother. It struck me that this affluent white woman reminded me so much of a Black mother in the projects. Then I remembered the stacks of Martha Stewart magazines and cookbooks that filled our home: Martha Stewart Living, Entertaining, Weddings, Better Homes, and Women's Day. My mother devoured them. She studied them like sacred texts, absorbing every detail and applying what she learned to our modest home.

She may have lived in Perry Homes, but she carried herself with the grace and precision of someone who believed in beauty, order, and possibility. Her home-making wasn't just survival; it was art. It was resistance. It was love.

CHAPTER 3
MY FATHER'S STORY

My Stepfather

While we were living in the Perry Homes Projects, my mother's cousin came to visit, and he brought along a friend. The man was handsome, though he walked with a pronounced limp due to polio in his left leg. He was quiet, shy, and inexperienced with women. But something about my mother caught his attention.

He didn't know how to approach her, so my mother took the lead. She saw his hesitation and gently opened the door to conversation. They connected quickly. When her cousin prepared to leave, my mother told him, "You can go, but your friend is staying here with me."

That moment marked the beginning of their relationship. For him, it was his first romantic experience, and it must have left a lasting impression because he never left. Not long after, my mother became pregnant with her fourth child.

Having already had three children out of wedlock, my mother wanted something different this time. The young man proposed, and she accepted. They were married at the courthouse one month before the baby was born.

He moved in with us while we were still in the projects. From the beginning, he asked my siblings and me to call him "Daddy," and he earned that title. He cared for us, provided for us, and treated us as his own. In many ways, he did more for us than our biological father ever had.

I respected him for that. In a place filled with instability and broken promises, he showed up and stayed. He owned a 1968 Grand Torino, and he would take my mother, brother, sister, and me for rides in it. I can still smell the black leather seats, hear the roar of the souped-up engine, and the joy he had in riding in that car. He brought a sense of stability to us. His presence brought a rare sense of consistency to our lives, and for that, I will always be grateful.

The High Price of Tupperware

There was an elderly woman who lived in our apartment building in Perry Homes. Every time she saw my mother, she invited us to attend a Bible study led by a man she called the "Man of God." My mother always declined, politely but firmly.

One evening, my mother decided to host a Tupperware party. She cooked a variety of dishes and needed containers to store the food. She knocked on the old lady's door and asked to borrow some Tupperware. The woman agreed, but only on one condition: that my mother attend the Bible study. Reluctantly, my mother accepted.

That Wednesday, we went to the study. The "Man of God" was preaching to a room full of young women, women just like my mother. He spoke with intensity, promising prosperity, protection, and deliverance from poverty if they submitted to God and to his leadership. His delivery was unlike anything my mother had ever heard. It was blunt, raw, even vulgar at times, yet undeniably captivating.

My mother had dropped out of school in the eighth grade. She was overwhelmed, raising three children alone and struggling to survive. Later, she confided in me that she had once considered ending her life, and ours, just to escape the pain. She was in a deeply vulnerable place when she joined the organization and surrendered herself to the teachings of the "Man of God."

At the time, she had just married my stepfather, a man with polio in his left leg and a stern, often belligerent demeanor. Despite his rough edges, he accepted my mother and her children without hesitation. He worked full-time at the Greyhound Bus Station and moonlighted as a shade-tree mechanic.

At Christmas, he transformed. He went all out to make the holidays magical, and my mother's Martha Stewart-inspired homemaking added warmth and charm to our modest home. Butter cookies, bowls of fruit and nuts, stockings on the fireplace, and Christmas music filled the air. Those memories are etched in my heart.

Though my stepfather was cold for most of the year, Christmas softened him. He became the man we wished he could be all the time. I had no relationship with my biological father, so it was easy to accept my stepfather as "Daddy."

But he was not happy about my mother's involvement with the "Man of God." The services often lasted all night, and my mother would leave at eight in the evening and return just before dawn. He demanded that she stop attending. She refused. When he slapped her across the face in anger, she stood her ground. Her resolve was unshaken.

Frustrated and confused, my stepfather decided to

attend a meeting himself. The "Man of God" welcomed him warmly and even gave him money to replace our broken refrigerator. That gesture won him over, and soon after, he joined the organization too.

My mother was praised for her "persecution," for enduring violence in order to follow the faith. Not only did she become a member, but she also brought her husband into the fold.

My stepfather's mechanical skills became vital to the ministry. The congregation was poor and could not afford car repairs. He fixed their vehicles for free, asking only that they pay for the parts. He never said no. Even after working two jobs, he would crawl out of bed in the middle of the night to help stranded members on the highway. I watched him limp through life with a polio-stricken leg, working harder than most able-bodied men.

He never legally adopted us, but he made us feel like we were his. From day one, he told us to call him "Daddy," and that is exactly who he became to me.

My mother and stepfather were completely devoted to the "Man of God's" ministry. Their loyalty was unwavering, and their sacrifices were many.

CHAPTER 4
LIFE INSIDE THE CULT

The Isolation

One of the first demands the "Man of God" made of my mother was that she sever all ties with her family. Anyone who wasn't a member of the organization was considered dangerous, an enemy of her spiritual connection. She was told that outsiders could corrupt her faith, and therefore, she must not only cut them off but also denounce them as evil.

This doctrine bred suspicion and fear. From the moment my mother joined the organization, she decided that her children would not know their grandparents, aunts, uncles, or cousins. I don't believe she fully understood the consequences of that choice. It left us without a sense of identity, disconnected from our roots, and emotionally isolated.

But there was a calculated reason behind it. When someone is cut off from their family, they become vulnerable, easier to control. The "Man of God" reinforced this belief by teaching that non-members were immoral and corrupt. He encouraged followers to confront their relatives with degrading accusations and ultimatums: either join the organization or be cast out.

Most family members, understandably, responded with hurt and rejection. "Goodbye and good riddance" became the common refrain. Occasionally, a relative would reach out, hoping to reconnect. But my mother, following the teachings she had embraced, would repeat the same rhetoric and close the door again.

After each encounter, she would report back to the "Man of God," who praised her for her boldness and loyalty. Her actions were celebrated publicly. She was asked to share her "testimony" before the congregation, and they responded with loud "Amens" and applause. The approval was intoxicating. It reinforced her choices and deepened her commitment.

I watched as the natural bonds of family were sacrificed for the fleeting reward of applause and validation. The "Man of God" used public praise as a powerful tool of control, turning loyalty into performance and isolation into virtue.

The Power of Confession

Brother Allen ruled with absolute authority. His leadership was built on fear, manipulation, and a carefully crafted image of spiritual indispensability. He often boasted that no one else could lead the organization as he did. Through sermons and private counsel, he planted seeds of insecurity in the hearts of his followers, convincing them that they were too weak, too broken, or too ignorant to survive without his guidance.

Leaving the church wasn't just discouraged; it was condemned. Anyone who walked away was told they were destined for failure, misery, and eternal damnation. Their children, too, were said to be doomed to suffer. This fear-based theology kept people tethered to the ministry, afraid to imagine life beyond its walls.

During church services, testimonies were closely monitored. Brother Allen expected to be honored explicitly in every story. He rejected titles like "Pastor," "Reverend," or "Bishop," teaching that true humility meant rejecting such labels. Citing Matthew 23:8–12, "But be not ye called Rabbi: for one is your Master, even Christ; and all ye are brethren"—he pointed out that the apostles referred to themselves simply by name: Paul, Peter, James. This teaching set him apart from other preachers and subtly implied that those who demanded titles were false prophets.

Another hallmark of Brother Allen's leadership was his public confession of sin. He modeled this after the approach used in Alcoholics Anonymous, where leaders share personal flaws to encourage openness. He taught that confession was essential for spiritual cleansing, quoting 1 John 1:9: "If we confess our sins, he is faithful and just to forgive us..."

Brother Allen led by example, confessing to adultery with a young woman in the congregation. He wept openly, expressing what he called "godly sorrow." But his confession came with a twist: he blamed the young woman for tempting him, accusing her of seductive behavior that led him astray. This deflection of responsibility was troubling, yet it didn't diminish his standing. On the contrary, it strengthened it. His vulnerability was seen as a strength, and his honesty was celebrated.

After his confession, he required the congregation to follow suit. Every member was expected to confess every sin they could remember, publicly and with visible remorse. If your confession didn't meet his standards of "godly sorrow," it was rejected. Without proper confession, you were told you could not be blessed.

The Theater of Confession

In the cult, confession wasn't about healing—it was about performance. Every member was expected to confess every sin they could remember. It wasn't enough to admit wrongdoing. You had to weep. You had to tremble. You had to bleed guilt from your pores.

If your confession didn't meet the Man of God's standards of "godly sorrow," it was rejected. He would say you were holding back. That your heart wasn't broken enough. That your repentance wasn't real. And without proper confession, you were told you could not be blessed. You were spiritually blocked. Cursed. Unworthy.

So people began to perform. They made up sins—fabricated stories of lust, rebellion, dishonor—just to satisfy his hunger for brokenness. Just to be seen. Just to be accepted. Just to survive.

It became a theater of shame. A ritual of humiliation. And the more dramatic your confession, the more spiritual you were considered to be. The more you cried, the more you were praised. The more you exposed yourself, the more you were "delivered."

But it wasn't deliverance. It was degradation.

We weren't being cleansed. We were being conditioned. Taught to equate pain with purity. Taught to distrust our own hearts. Taught to believe that God only loved us when we were broken and bleeding.

And long after we left, that belief lingered. It still does.

As a child, I was captivated by Brother Allen's ability

to admit his faults. Unlike televangelists who were exposed by scandal, he seemed to volunteer his truth. That transparency made him appear more trustworthy, more powerful. But in hindsight, I see that confession was used not to heal, but to control.

The Cult of Honor and Control

Brother Allen trained every member in the proper format for giving a testimony. It always began the same way: "I give honor to God, his son Jesus, and my Pastor, Brother Allen." From there, you were expected to describe how your life had been a complete failure until you met him. The message was clear: your worth, your salvation, and your success were all tied to your relationship with Brother Allen.

It wasn't that no one else had the mental capacity to lead the congregation. It was that no one else had the ability to manipulate it the way he did. For years, he conditioned us to recognize his importance in every aspect of our lives. His name had to be mentioned in every prayer, every testimony, every conversation. If you failed to honor him properly, you were told that God did not accept you and that you were displeasing in His sight.

Every Bible study, every church service, and every gathering reinforced this idea. Brother Allen became the focal point of our spiritual lives, not Christ, not scripture, but him. Our goal was no longer to seek divine truth, but to win his approval.

He also enforced a strict dress code for women and girls. Dresses and skirts had to reach the ankles and could not be form-fitting. Makeup was forbidden because it was said to enhance "sinful features." Women were blamed for any lustful thoughts men might have about them, and the burden of purity was placed entirely on their shoulders.

Leadership roles were reserved for men. Women were taught that their divine purpose was to be wives and mothers, nothing more. While I believe being a wife and mother are among the most important roles a woman can hold, I also know that women are capable of much more.

Some of the best teachers I had in school were women. Some of the most brilliant doctors, lawyers, scientists, and business leaders in the world are women. Some of the most effective world leaders are women. Scripture itself honors women in profound ways. After Jesus was crucified, He first appeared to women and instructed them to tell the disciples to meet Him in Galilee. The woman with the alabaster box poured precious ointment on Jesus, and He declared that wherever the gospel is preached, her act of devotion would be remembered.

These truths stand in stark contrast to the teachings we received. Brother Allen's doctrine diminished women, while scripture elevated them. His control was not just spiritual; it was psychological, emotional, and deeply personal.

The Roots of Misogyny

Brother Allen's treatment of women often felt rooted in something deeper than doctrine; it felt personal. Over time, I came to believe that his disdain for women stemmed from a traumatic experience in his childhood.

As the story goes, when Allen was a young boy, he noticed one day that his mother was missing from the house. Concerned, he went searching for her. He wandered into the wooded area near their home and stumbled upon a scene that would leave a lasting scar: his mother was engaged in a sexual affair with another woman's husband from the neighborhood.

Witnessing this betrayal of his father shattered something in him. The image of his mother in that moment, caught in an act of infidelity, seemed to shape his perception of women for the rest of his life. From that point on, he viewed women as untrustworthy, morally weak, and beneath men. He believed they were incapable of holding positions of leadership or authority over men.

This early trauma appeared to fuel the rigid gender roles and harsh teachings he later imposed on his congregation. His doctrine wasn't just about spiritual discipline; it was about control. And for women, that control was absolute.

Fear and Favor

Brother Allen's psychological control was unmatched, but he didn't rely on mental manipulation alone. He reinforced it with physical punishment. Children weren't the only ones subjected to beatings; grown men and women were also publicly disciplined.

I'll never forget one incident. A woman complained to Brother Allen that her husband spent more time watching and playing sports than he did with her and their ten children. During a church service, Brother Allen confronted the man before the entire congregation. The husband explained that he loved his family but also enjoyed sports and competition. That explanation didn't satisfy the "Man of God."

Without hesitation, Brother Allen ordered two men to seize him. A third man beat him with a belt in front of his wife, his children, and the entire congregation. Afterward, Brother Allen forbade him from ever participating in sports again.

This man wasn't lazy or irresponsible. He was a hardworking provider who had held a city job for over twenty years. Watching him humiliated and physically punished shook me to my core. I remember thinking, "What have we gotten ourselves into?" The fear was immediate and overwhelming. But there was also a strange sense of awe—how could one man wield so much power that he could have another man beaten in public without resistance?

Fear and wonder. That combination is potent when used by someone in authority, especially a cult leader.

As a young boy, I often asked myself, Of all the kids in the world, how did I end up here? I felt cursed. Yet I also felt conflicted. I feared Brother Allen, but I also believed in him. He was charismatic and knew how to make you feel seen. He had a way of making you believe you were the only person in the room.

People who seek control often present themselves as kind and approachable at first. I wasn't the best-looking kid, nor did I have a magnetic personality. I was an extreme introvert with low self-esteem. Tall, lanky, and painfully skinny, my mother struggled to find clothes that fit me. Most people looked past me. Besides my mother, I felt invisible.

But as I grew older, my features changed. My body caught up with my head, and I began to look more balanced. I also started to show signs of intelligence and quick learning. That's when Brother Allen began to take notice. He told me I was one of the smartest kids in the congregation and praised my ability to learn faster than others.

That recognition meant everything to me. It drew me closer to him and deepened my admiration. I became fanatically devoted to his teachings. But even then, I sensed something wasn't quite right. I never felt like he truly liked me.

Brother Allen had a pattern. When he saw someone, male or female, with natural gifts, he would use them. But he also made sure they never felt equal to him. He'd find subtle ways to demean their character, to keep them humble, to remind them who held the power.

Alongside Brother Allen's charismatic bedside manner was an arrogant darkness that mirrored the attitude of a white slave master toward his slaves. The slave master viewed his slaves as inferior, not even human, but his property. He manifested and solidified this belief by calling the slave a "Nigger." When they used that word, they meant you were on the same level as a dog. In fact, they treated their dogs better. The "Man of God" dealt with his members in the same fashion. He felt they were degenerates and beneath him and often referred to them as "Niggers" or "Dummies."

The irony was striking. The "Man of God" was a Black man of African American descent. He came from the same generation that experienced racial injustice and oppression from white America. Yet he dealt with his own congregation in the same dehumanizing manner. I remember witnessing him call us "niggers," and it felt no different from hearing a racist white man say it. You couldn't call him racist because he was a Black man. It was a deeply confusing feeling.

That is why, when I hear rappers use the word "nigger" in their songs, it disturbs my soul. I know the origin of that word, and I experienced the feeling of being called one by someone intent on breaking the spirit of his own people. The "Man of God" used it to oppress his congregation and emasculate the men and women to prove dominance.

During slavery, white masters were determined to keep their "niggers" from learning to read or becoming educated. They wanted to keep them ignorant to maintain control. They were so afraid of an educated Black person that, if they discovered one could read, they might punish him inhumanely—by plucking out an eye, hobbling him, or even castrating him. Keeping the slave ignorant was essential to keeping him enslaved.

Brother Allen shared this same mentality. He believed most of the children in his organization only needed an education up to the sixth grade. He didn't promote higher education among his members. If anyone displayed intelligence or insight, the "Man of God" labeled them "high-minded" and made a concentrated effort to shame or suppress them. He seemed fearful or intimidated by intelligent members, viewing them as threats to his authority and control.

This, too, was another trait Brother Allen shared with the white slave master.

PART II
ENTERING THE CULT

CHAPTER 5
THE MACHINERY OF CONTROL

My Oldest Brother

My mother had her first child at just sixteen years old. My oldest brother, David Lenard Shockley Jr., was born on March 26, 1971. He was a beautiful baby with striking eyes and a magnetic personality. Intelligent and outgoing, David had the chance to bond with both sides of our family before my mother met the "Man of God."

When she joined the organization, David quickly became one of the "Man of God's" favorites among the children. But he had a rebellious streak. He questioned authority, and that made him both admired and watched.

I also had a younger sister—just a year and a half younger than me—who was bright, beautiful, and quick-witted. Our father, an officer in the United States Air Force, was a highly intelligent man, and he passed that intelligence down to all of us. But there was something my siblings inherited that I didn't: lighter skin and conventional good looks.

I was dark-skinned, introverted, and not considered attractive by the standards of the community we were in. The "Man of God" had a clear preference for lighter-skinned, good-looking members, especially women. That bias was obvious, and it shaped how we were treated.

He even questioned whether I shared the same father as my siblings. Because I looked different, he accused my mother of promiscuity, insisting she didn't know who my father was. My mother stood firm, insisting that all her children had the same father. But the "Man of God" repeated his accusations so often and so convincingly that even she began to doubt herself.

Before we met him, there was no question about my paternity. My father claimed me as his son. But the "Man of God" believed he knew better than everyone else. He used this rhetoric to manipulate my mother, to shame her, and to maintain control over her and her children.

This created a hierarchy among us. My brother—light-skinned, handsome, intelligent, and "legitimate"—was favored. My sister, too, was admired. I, on the other hand, was treated as less-than. I experienced discrimination from the people closest to me, rooted in the teachings of a man I had come to revere.

As a child, I didn't have the wisdom or life experience to recognize what was happening. The "Man of God" was clever in how he delivered this environment of favoritism and shame. He liked me, but he liked my siblings more. And I accepted that.

If you're wondering what filled those long, marathon church meetings, this is an example. Rhetoric like this—personal, invasive, and manipulative—was preached for hours. Each member of the congregation had their own version of this treatment. It was the kind of doctrine that oppressed my mother for years and eroded whatever self-esteem she had left after being abandoned with three children by the man she once trusted.

My Oldest Brother's Escape

My oldest brother, David Lenard Shockley Jr., was fair-skinned with red hair, striking features, and a sharp mind. He stood out among the young men in the congregation and quickly became one of the "Man of God's" favorites. But admiration in that world was never simple.

The "Man of God" didn't just like or dislike people—he compartmentalized them. He could admire your intelligence while resenting your independence. He could praise your talents while quietly plotting to keep you in check. That was the dynamic between him and my brother.

He often labeled intelligent members as "high-minded," a term pulled from 2 Timothy 3, which warns of pride and arrogance in the last days. But in our congregation, "high-minded" became a weapon. It was used to shame, isolate, and control anyone who showed promise. Once you were labeled, your days were numbered—or your life in the organization would be filled with hardship.

My brother was intelligent, confident, and strong-willed. That made him a threat.

One day, he had a disagreement with a young woman in the congregation—someone known for stirring trouble. The situation escalated into a physical altercation. The "Man of God" sided with the young woman and ordered four men to beat my brother. They took him to a secluded location, and though he fought back, a fifteen-year-old boy stood no chance against grown men.

That beating was a turning point. My brother had tried to run away before, but my mother found him and punished him for it. Still, his resolve never wavered. Once he made up his mind, it was as good as done.

He came to me and asked if I wanted to go with him. I was only eleven. I liked my bed, my meals, and the warmth of our home. I asked him, "Where are you going, and where would we live?" He answered, "I don't know, brother, but I'm leaving." I told him no. Looking back, I think he had a plan but didn't want to risk sharing it. I don't blame him.

Though I didn't go with him, I gave him the only support I could—about two dollars in change I had saved. It wasn't much, but it was my way of saying, "I believe in you."

My brother left. He chose freedom. He went on to serve honorably in the United States Army. He built a life, a legacy, and left behind an inheritance for his children and grandchildren. As Proverbs 13:22 says, "A good man leaveth an inheritance to his children's children." My brother did that.

He passed away on January 6, 2020, and was laid to rest at the military burial grounds in Canton, Georgia. His life was a testament to courage, resilience, and the power of choosing your own path—even when the odds are stacked against you.

Mary Allen – A Light in the Darkness

During his reign at The House of Prayer, the "Man of God" was married to a woman named Mary Allen, his second wife. He had long abandoned his first wife, with whom he had two children, before ever becoming a pastor. I never met his first wife, so I can't speak to her character. All I knew were the stories he told, and I've learned firsthand how easily he could twist a narrative to destroy someone's reputation if they crossed him.

According to him, he met his first wife in Los Angeles when they were young. She was beautiful, and he pursued her relentlessly. She refused to have sex before marriage, holding firm to her convictions, claiming to be a virgin. Eventually, he proposed, and she accepted. But on their wedding night, he claimed the experience didn't meet his expectations and accused her of lying about her virginity. The relationship quickly unraveled, ending in divorce and allegations of infidelity —though we only ever heard his side.

By the time my mother joined the organization, the "Man of God" was married to Mary Allen. This woman, I knew personally. And I can say without hesitation: she may have been one of the sweetest people I've ever met.

Mary came from a wholesome, loving background, very different from the man she married. In my opinion, she was too good for him. He was only able to marry her because her family respected his father, who was a preacher. That connection gave him credibility in their eyes.

Mary had a gentle spirit. She used to sing a song before the congregation called "I'm Standing in the Safety Zone." Her voice wasn't as strong as my mother's, but when she sang, you could feel the spirit move. The lyrics still echo in my mind:

"While strolling along life's highway, there arose a mighty storm

And I heard a voice from heaven say you're standing out there alone..."

She sang of loss, perseverance, and stepping into the safety zone of faith. I didn't realize at the time how real those words would become in my own life.

Mary made me feel seen. She often told me she felt like I was her son, and that meant the world to me. Her kindness was rare, and her Lemon Meringue pie was unforgettable—sweet, just like her. There are a few people in life about whom you can honestly say, "I have nothing bad to say". Mary Allen was one of those people.

Lessons from the Lake and the Land

The "Man of God" was a landscaper by trade, and he worked for himself. As a kid, he would drive across town to pick me up, along with other young boys from the congregation, to help him with jobs. Most of us were barely teenagers, some as young as twelve. He said he liked taking me because I was a hard worker and didn't mind getting dirty.

We spent long days in affluent neighborhoods laying sod, planting bushes, and building flower beds. It was tough work, but I learned a lot—skills I still use today. More than that, I learned the value of hard work and the pride that comes from doing a job well.

Beyond landscaping, the "Man of God" also took us fishing in the woods. It was usually fun—until the day I got separated from the group. I wandered too far and suddenly realized I was lost. I couldn't tell which direction I was going: north, south, east, or west. Panic set in.

Then I encountered a dog. It was large and aggressive, barking furiously. I ran, expecting it to chase me, but by some miracle, it didn't. Even in that terrifying moment, I felt protected—as if God or a guardian angel was watching over me. I truly believed I was not alone.

Eventually, I found a creek and heard someone calling my name. I shouted back and followed the voices until I was reunited with the group. That day taught me something valuable: if you're ever lost in the woods, find water—it will likely lead you back to civilization.

Despite that scare, I still loved those trips. The "Man of God" often organized road trips for the congregation to state parks with lakes and picnic areas. We visited Chickamauga Lake in Tennessee, the Cherokee Reservation in North Carolina, Jacksonville, Florida, and most often, Allatoona Lake in Georgia, just a short drive from Atlanta.

Allatoona Lake was dirty, but we didn't care. The men would scout out safe swimming spots, checking for rocks and drop-offs. Once they gave the green light, we'd run and jump in with excitement.

One time, we found a giant boulder in the middle of the lake and decided to use it as a diving board. When my turn came, I climbed up and did my best Greg Louganis swan dive. It felt graceful—until I hit something underwater. I didn't feel much pain, just a bump. But when I surfaced, a girl—ironically, the same one who'd fought with my brother—screamed, "Oh my God! You've got a piece of meat hanging out of your head!"

I touched my head and saw blood on my hand. Her reaction scared me more than the injury itself. I cried and ran to find my mom. That dive led to a long ride from Allatoona Lake to Grady Hospital. My mother kept me awake the whole way, afraid I'd slip into a coma. I was exhausted, but I stayed alert.

Thirteen stitches and a bottle of ibuprofen later, I had a new scar—and a new respect for lake diving. But it didn't stop me from loving those trips. I always looked forward to them. The lake, the laughter, the freedom—it was a bright spot in a complicated childhood.

Invisible Chains

The "Man of God" always had to be the center of attention—no matter the occasion. Even at the park, where families came to relax and enjoy nature, he demanded that everyone gather around him and listen for hours. If you walked away to enjoy the scenery or play with your children, he would chastise you publicly, accusing you of not loving God or the things of God.

He used the name of God to ensure that he remained the focal point. Every gathering—whether a church service or a picnic—became a stage for his authority.

We met three times a week for marathon church services. But that wasn't enough. He also scheduled "Recreation" three times a week—supposedly a time for fellowship and fun. We'd play spades and board games, and for a while, it was genuinely enjoyable.

Until he arrived.

Once the "Man of God" showed up, recreation transformed into another sermon. He'd call everyone to gather around him, and suddenly, we were back in church—whether we wanted to be or not.

You dared not skip these gatherings. If you did, he'd assassinate your character in front of your wife, children, and friends. He'd say you didn't care about God. He'd ask, "How could you not want to sit at the feet of the Man of God and hear the word every chance you get?"

I sat through countless hours of preaching against my will—not because I believed, but because I feared the consequences. The stigma of being "unspiritual," the embarrassment, the judgment from my own family—it was too much to bear.

Fear was his most effective weapon:

- Fear of Hell if you questioned him
- Fear of being labeled a Judas
- Fear of excommunication—from the church, your friends, even your own family

He had us bound—not with chains, but with guilt. Not with gates, but with shame. Not with locks, but with fear.

People accused him of leading a cult. He'd respond mockingly, "If this is a cult, then where are the chains? Where are the gates and locks?"

But the chains were real. They were mental—invisible to the eye, but heavy on the soul. And every link in those chains was forged in the name of God.

Earlier, I shared my earliest memory—my fourth birthday, celebrated with my cousin and aunt. That day was joyful, but it was also the last time I saw them. If I passed them on the street today, I wouldn't recognize them. That's how complete the separation was.

Growing up without knowing your grandparents, aunts, uncles, or cousins leaves a person with no sense of identity. When someone is encouraged—or required—to sever family ties, they become vulnerable. Easier to mold. Easier to control.

The "Man of God" made it clear: outside influences were dangerous. Family members were labeled as worldly, ungodly, even enemies of the faith. He quoted scripture to reinforce this, saying, "He that is a friend of the world is the enemy of God." To remain in good standing, we were told to cut off all ties.

Once you accepted that, once you pledged allegiance to him in the name of Jesus, he became the one who defined your worth. Your past was rewritten. Your lineage was degraded. He would speak harshly about members' families, using language meant to shame and dehumanize. It was a tactic to elevate himself while diminishing everyone else.

Even when he confessed his own mistakes, they were framed as noble missteps—or the fault of others. He once admitted to having a relationship with a young woman in the church, but claimed she had seduced him while he was trying to help her. When asked about the pain this caused his wife, he said she deserved it because of her own sins.

His confessions were never equal to ours. He had a way of minimizing his wrongs while magnifying ours. And when it came to that young woman—who was still a teenager—his behavior crossed boundaries that should never be crossed. She was vulnerable, and instead of protecting her, he exerted control. When she showed interest in someone her own age, he responded with jealousy and punishment.

These moments weren't isolated. They were part of a pattern—one that blurred the lines between spiritual leadership and personal domination. And while there were no physical chains, the mental ones were real—invisible, but binding. Installed in the name of God.

Somehow, whenever the Man of God tells something that he did wrong, he has a way of making it not seem so bad. Not as bad or dirty as your sins that you committed. He will confess a sin, then whitewash it with an excuse as to why he committed the sin, but the devil, as they say, is in the details. This young woman, whom the man of God claimed seduced him, was only 17 years old and still a virgin when the man of God betrayed his wife and started having sex with her. The man of God was obsessed with this young woman and even beat her with a belt because she was showing attention to a young man who was her age, who was also a member of the congregation. The man of God would take the young woman under his house in the basement and have sex with her, and his wife would hear them in the basement having sex.

When his wife confronted him through tears about the affair, he coldly told her to get away from him with all that crying, saying she deserved to be hurt for her own sins.

After maintaining the affair for a couple of years, he arranged for the young woman to marry a new member of the congregation because of a pregnancy scare. When she later gave birth to her first child, people whispered about who the father really was — her husband or the Man of God.

There was never a DNA test, but the Man of God quickly shaped the story, insisting the baby belonged to her husband. The truth, however, was never proven and remains uncertain to this day.

Even after her marriage, the Man of God continued his sexual relationship with her for at least another three years.

His public confession was that he "fell" and had sex with a young woman in the church, told as if it were a single, regrettable incident. But what he didn't admit was that it was a five-year affair, half of which took place while she was married. During that time, he continuously betrayed his wife and disrespected her in front of everyone who knew the truth.

I won't divulge how I found out these details, but let's just say the source is very reliable.

Eventually, the young woman left the Man of God's congregation, but he did not let her go easily. He sent one of his main members to drive down to Florida and bring her back. During the return trip, while the member drove, the Man of God engaged in sex with the young woman in the back seat.

The Man of God is very careful not to allow members to minimize or excuse their sins as he does his own. In fact, he puts a magnifying glass on the sins of others, sometimes making them appear larger than they really are. He demands that members go into detail when confessing, and if you leave out even the smallest thing, he accuses you of being dishonest.

To a newcomer, the Man of God seems like the most honest and humble person you could ever meet. He knows how to create an illusion of humility while still sending the message that he is somehow more special, more chosen, than everyone else. That's how he gets you to open up to him—to trust him with your deepest, darkest secrets.

He makes you feel safe. You feel like you can tell him anything. But once you've poured out your soul, he uses those same secrets to control you.

He even uses Scripture to persuade members to confess, quoting verses like, "If we confess our sins, he is faithful and just to forgive us our sins and cleanse us from all unrighteousness." What he fails to explain is that the "He" in that Scripture is **God**—and only God. God is the one we are called to confess to, unless He directs us otherwise. Only God can forgive, and only God can cleanse us of all unrighteousness. He is also the only one who truly understands why we do the things we do. God considers the whole matter, not just the act itself, but the heart and the struggle behind it.

Shame as a Weapon

The Man of God taught something very different from grace. In his world, confession wasn't about healing—it was about control. He demanded that every member confess their sins directly to him, no matter how distant or innocent. Even things done as children. Even things we barely understood.

I remember confessing to him something that happened when I was five years old. A young girl—also five—and I engaged in a sexual act we couldn't possibly comprehend. We were just kids. Curious. Unaware. But in that moment of confession, I wasn't met with compassion. I was branded.

From that day forward, I carried a label ("Pussy Lips"), a name meant to humiliate me, to reduce me, to keep me bound. That label wasn't just cruel. It was a sentence. A reminder that in this cult, your past was never forgiven. It was weaponized.

Both that girl and I grew up in the organization. And though we were wrong for engaging in such an act, we were children. Children who somehow knew about something far too grown-up. And that's what haunts me most—not just what we did, but how we knew. What kind of environment teaches five-year-olds about oral sex? What kind of system fails to protect innocence and then punishes it?

I've carried that moment with me for years. Not just the memory, but the shame. The confusion. The question: Was I ever really a child? Or was I just another soul waiting to be broken?

I answer this question by taking into consideration that growing up in the organization as a child, all you hear is very detailed and graphic conversations about sex, oral sex, and homosexuality.

These subjects should never be introduced to a child, because children are not mature enough to properly process such information. Pastor Leon Owens of New Life in Christ Church in Atlanta teaches that when God created Adam and Eve, He placed a certain tree in the midst of the Garden of Eden—the Tree of the Knowledge of Good and Evil—and forbade them to eat from it.

Now, why would God create this tree if He never

intended for them to eat from it? Pastor Owens teaches and believes that eventually God would have allowed Adam and Eve to eat from the tree, but only at the right time—when they were mature enough to handle being exposed to its knowledge and able to properly process what it represented. If God was never going to let them eat from the tree, then why create it in the first place? Pastor Owens believes God intended for them to partake of it eventually, when the time was right.

I believe the same principle applies to raising a child. Certain topics should never be discussed or introduced until the child's mind is mature enough to process them with understanding. Unfortunately, the Man of God does not share this belief.

As a child, I constantly heard the Man of God talking about topics such as "eating pussy", "sucking dicks", "putting your dick in pussy", "men sticking their dicks in a woman's ass", men and women licking each other's asses, and the list goes on and on! Now, if this is all a child hears for hours upon hours, eventually some—if not all—of those children are going to try some of the things they've been hearing about. This organization breeds that kind of behavior. Once you act out the things you've constantly heard, the Man of God makes you confess them to him. And once you confess, he uses that information to control you.

The Man of God has a way of magnifying your

wrongdoings and making you feel like one of the most evil people in the world. If you ever challenge him on any matter, he will use those same sinful secrets you confided in him to assassinate your character and destroy your credibility with your wife, children, and other members of the church. Your family and fellow members will lose respect for you.

One thing that the Man of God hated was to be challenged by a member of the church on any matter. You could clearly see where he was wrong on the matter, but you had better learn to shut up! In the organization, you had to learn to "go along to get along". Unless you were willing to pay the price of being "hazed". He will have your own children assisting him in this character assassination or breakdown. It is like a character "break down" session or a "hazing". By the time he is finished with you, you will know not to ever challenge him on anything, whether he is right or wrong. And before you know it, you will feel like nothing more than a "brainwashed puppet," and the Man of God is the puppet master. This is a very effective way to exude control over a group of people. I cannot tell you how many people I have witnessed the Man of God break down in this manner.

The Approval That Never Came

Most of my life revolved around two things: marathon church meetings led by the "Man of God" and weekend trips to state parks and lakes. But those meetings—what I call marathon church meetings—were unlike anything most people could imagine.

They often lasted twelve to twenty-four hours, sometimes even longer. These weren't traditional Bible studies. The Bible was rarely opened. Instead, they were sessions of psychological conditioning, where hunger and sleep deprivation were used to break us down and reshape our thinking.

In those meetings, we were groomed to crave one thing above all else: the approval of the "Man of God." His approval became synonymous with God's approval. If he accepted you, you believed Heaven did too. If he rejected you, you feared you were damned.

That kind of dynamic is powerful and deeply confusing. When someone positions themselves as the gatekeeper to divine favor, it distorts your sense of worth, your choices, and your connection to something greater than yourself.

I wanted his approval more than anything. And I wasn't alone. The desire to be accepted—especially in a spiritual context—is one of the strongest forces in human life. But no matter how hard I tried, no matter what I sacrificed, I could never win it.

I was more loyal to the "Man of God" than I was to my mother, my father, my siblings, my wife, or even my children. Yet it was never enough. I spent thirty-four years in his cult, from the age of three until thirty-seven, and I never earned his approval.

Love Held Hostage

Even in my marriage, I couldn't find acceptance.

My wife and I had twelve children together—a life built on shared history, shared faith, and shared responsibility. But love was never truly ours. Her approval was tied directly to his. The Man of God. The one who stood between me and every meaningful relationship in my life.

If I didn't please him, I couldn't please her. If I didn't win his favor, I couldn't win hers. And I never did. No matter how hard I tried, no matter how obedient I became, I was never enough for him. Which meant I was never enough for her either.

He was the gatekeeper—not just to spiritual blessings, but to emotional connection. To my wife's approval. To my children's respect. To the congregation's acceptance. Everything flowed through him. And if he shut the gate, you were left outside. Alone.

I lived in that loneliness. I raised children in that loneliness. I worshipped in that loneliness. And the cruelest part was that it didn't feel like abandonment—it felt like punishment. Like I had failed God, and this was the price.

But it wasn't God. It was him.

And now, as I look back, I realize how much of my life was spent chasing approval that was never mine to earn. How many moments of joy were stolen. How many relationships were strained. How many years were lost.

Love should never be held hostage. But in the cult, it was.

That realization was one of the hardest truths I've had to face. I gave everything—my time, my loyalty, my identity—and still came up short. But in that emptiness, I began to see the cracks in the foundation. And through those cracks, light eventually found its way in.

CHAPTER 6
CHILDHOOD WITHIN THE WALLS

The Sound Before the Storm

The "Man of God" did not allow eating during his services, no matter how long they lasted. As children, we had to ask permission just to drink a glass of water. I learned to sneak into the bathroom, cup my hands under the faucet, and steal a sip. When you grow up in an environment where even basic needs are restricted, you learn to be sneaky just to survive.

These meetings usually began around eight o'clock in the evening, but the "Man of God" rarely arrived before midnight. In his mind, the service didn't truly begin until he walked in. Until then, we followed a strict order of service.

Devotional service came first. Two men would

stand before the congregation, leading us in song and prayer. One would kneel at the altar to pray, followed by another song. During the singing, the men would raise their hands, signaling the congregation to stand and inviting someone to come forward and pray. It became a race—whoever reached the altar first got to pray. I saw many people start toward the front only to turn back, beaten to the spot.

After three songs and three prayers, devotional service would close, and testimony service would begin. A brother would start with a song:

"I believe I'll testify while I have a chance, because I may not have this chance anymore..."

Then someone would jump up and begin testifying.

Every testimony began the same way: "I give honor to God and his son Jesus Christ, and I give honor to the Man of God and his wife." After that, they'd speak about how good the "Man of God" had been to them. Recognition of him was mandatory—no exceptions.

After a few testimonies, the choir would sing three or four songs, followed by a soloist. My mother was the lead soloist. And she could really sing.

I wish her performances had been recorded. I played piano at the church, and she was my favorite person to accompany. Her voice was full of passion and power. When she sang, she commanded the room. Even the

"Man of God," who rarely praised her, had to admit she had a gift.

Whenever we visited another church or had guests, he would call on her to sing—putting her on display like a prized jewel. I didn't hear many kind words from him about my mother, but her singing was the one thing he couldn't deny.

Her style reminded me of Mahalia Jackson, the legendary gospel singer of the civil rights era. Mahalia's voice was so moving that she was often asked to sing before Martin Luther King Jr. delivered his speeches. My mother's voice carried that same spirit. She was called upon often to sing before the "Man of God" arrived, warming the room with her gift.

Whenever she sang, I sat up straighter. I felt proud, amazed, and deeply moved. She sometimes sang up to three songs in a row, and each one stirred the soul.

By the time all this had taken place, hours had passed. The "Man of God" still hadn't arrived. But we waited, because in his eyes, nothing truly began until he walked through the door.

When God Arrived Late

The "Man of God" was rarely on time for anything. Services would begin around eight o'clock in the evening, but he often wouldn't arrive until midnight or later. And in his mind, the service didn't truly begin until he walked through the door.

There was no assistant pastor, no one officially designated to preach in his absence. So the Church Administrator, second in command, would do his best to hold the congregation's attention until the "Man of God" arrived. Most nights, he would preach or minister—not because he was called to, but because someone had to fill the void.

Sometimes, the Administrator would open the floor to other men in the congregation. One young man stood out. He was intelligent, charismatic, and good-looking, with a beautiful singing voice. He dreamed of becoming a minister, and I admired him deeply. His delivery was compelling, and he had that rare ability to hold a room.

In the Black church tradition, that combination—looks, voice, and oratory—is a recipe for success. The congregation responded to him with enthusiasm. He brought energy, clarity, and hope. But his gifts also cast a shadow over the "Man of God," whose delivery was less refined and whose voice lacked the same resonance.

By the time the "Man of God" finally arrived, the congregation was exhausted. People had been sitting for hours—some with jobs to go to the next morning, children to care for, and lives to live. But in his mind, the service was just beginning.

Permission to Leave

Leaving wasn't simple.

You couldn't just walk out. You had to raise your hand, wait to be acknowledged, and ask permission: "May I be excused?" And even then, it wasn't guaranteed. He might let you go—or he might not. It depended entirely on his mood, his judgment, his sense of control.

If you asked to leave, he'd challenge you. "Why do you want to leave? What place is better than the House of God?" In his view, his arrival marked the arrival of God. His presence was divine. His voice was sacred. And if you wanted to leave while he was speaking, you weren't just walking out of a room—you were walking out on God.

That kind of manipulation runs deep. It teaches you that your instincts are sinful. That your boundaries are rebellion. That your desire for rest, for space, for autonomy is a spiritual defect.

So you stay. You sit in discomfort. You silence your body's needs. You betray your own voice just to stay in his favor.

And over time, you forget that you ever had the right to leave.

Even if you'd already been there for four or five hours, your time meant nothing. If your excuse didn't meet his standards, he'd chastise you publicly, making you feel guilty, embarrassed, and spiritually weak.

Parents who wanted to take their children home for school the next day were told, "I don't care if these kids go to school or not—they need to hear what I've got to say." He'd claim that without his message, they'd grow up to be "whores and degenerates." He accused anyone who wanted to leave of loving the world more than they loved God.

Witnessing these moments, I often felt he was overstepping. But I kept those thoughts buried. I knew what happened to people who challenged him—ostracism, humiliation, and isolation. So I learned to suppress my instincts. I learned to go along to get along.

Over the years, I watched him demand more and more control. I saw it happening. I felt it happening. But I didn't know how to stop it. I was trapped in a system where obedience meant survival, and questioning meant betrayal.

The House That Wasn't Allowed

There was a young married couple in the congregation who had about ten children at the time. They lived in a cramped two-bedroom, one-bathroom apartment—rented from the "Man of God." Their living conditions were tight, and they dreamed of owning a home that could finally accommodate their growing family.

In 2008, when the housing market crashed, foreclosures flooded Atlanta. Homes that had once been out of reach were suddenly affordable. It was a rare moment of opportunity for poor families—if they had the means and the courage to act.

This couple found a beautiful two-story home with four or five bedrooms, listed by the bank for just $16,000. They had saved $12,000 and needed only $4,000 more. They turned to family members—also part of the congregation—and borrowed the remaining amount.

Everyone was thrilled. It felt like a miracle—a chance for this family to finally have space, dignity, and ownership.

Everyone, that is, except the "Man of God."

When he found out, he was furious. He demanded to know why he hadn't been consulted. He declared that no decision of such magnitude should be made without his approval. He chastised the family members who had loaned the money and planted seeds of guilt and doubt, suggesting they take the money back.

Then, in a dramatic display, he broke down crying before the entire congregation. He said he felt betrayed—not just by the couple, but by anyone who had helped them. His tears weren't about their well-being; they were about his authority.

The couple, overwhelmed and apologetic, let the opportunity slip away. They stayed in the same overcrowded apartment, still renting from the "Man of God." Years later, they had nineteen children—and still no home of their own.

The message was clear: no houses were to be bought, no cars purchased, no money exchanged—without his knowledge and approval. Every decision had to go through him.

I couldn't help but suspect that his outrage wasn't just about control—it was about income. If they bought their own home, they lost a tenant. He lost rent. He lost leverage.

This wasn't just spiritual leadership. It was economic entrapment.

I saw the pattern. I saw the power grab. But I felt powerless to stop it. So, like many others, I learned to stay quiet. I learned to go along to get along.

Witness to Control

Recently, a woman in the House of Prayer congregation —already a mother of thirteen children and expecting her fourteenth—found herself at odds with the "Man of God." She and her husband were longtime members of the organization. When she voiced disagreement over a matter in the church, the response was swift and deeply disturbing.

The "Man of God" threatened her with physical punishment, suggesting that the men of the church should discipline her. Then, in front of the entire congregation—including her husband, children, and mother—he allowed her own mother to publicly strike her. Her husband, instead of defending her, turned on her in anger and shouted, "Don't you ever disagree with the Man of God again!"

This wasn't an isolated incident. I had witnessed this kind of behavior since I was five years old. It was part of a culture where dissent was punished, and loyalty was demanded at all costs. Public shaming, verbal threats, and emotional manipulation were used to maintain control.

For years, I lived in that environment—watching people silenced, watching families torn between faith and fear. It took me decades to find the strength to leave. But I did. And now, I speak not just for myself, but for all those still trying to find their voice.

The Weight of Secrets

The Bible says, "When I was a child, I spoke as a child, I understood as a child, I thought as a child; but when I became a man, I put away childish things." (I Corinthians 13:11)

I hear God speaking to me through this scripture. I hear Him saying, I understand you may have done foolish things as a child, but when you grow, when you put those things away, I will forgive you.

That promise of grace has stayed with me. But as a member of the organization, I often found myself asking, Oh God, when? When will I be forgiven for things I did when I was five years old? Things I had long since let go—yet the "Man of God" and others in the congregation still held them against me.

I remember something the "Man of God" once said: "If you hold something over somebody's head, they won't go anywhere."

I've thought about that line for years. Why did he say that to me? Was he grooming me to follow in his footsteps—to carry the same tools of control? Did he want me to inherit his role, to become the next wielder of secrets and shame? Or was it pride—a need to show off how clever he was?

In that organization, every member had something hanging over them—a mistake, a confession, a moment of vulnerability. And the saddest part? We gave those secrets to him ourselves, believing we were seeking healing, not handing over leverage.

He didn't need chains. He didn't need locks. He held

people in place with memory, guilt, and fear. And the longer I stayed, the more I realized: forgiveness wasn't withheld by God. It was withheld by man.

Two Worlds in Conflict

Education was never a priority in the organization I was raised. School was treated as a legal obligation, not a path to growth. My mother enrolled us only because the law required it. The "Man of God" often dismissed formal education, saying that all a child needed were the "three R's"—Reading, 'Riting, and 'Rithmetic. I truly believe that if there had been a way to keep us out of school without facing legal consequences, we would have never gone.

Looking back, I feel a deep sadness about the lack of support I received. I had a natural ability to learn, but it was never nurtured. I remember showing up to school in worn clothes and shoes, feeling neglected and out of place. My classmates looked clean, well-groomed, and happy. I felt like I was inside a box, watching the world from behind glass.

There were so many rules that set us apart and made us targets. One of them was refusing to stand for the Pledge of Allegiance. Every morning at school, students were asked to stand and recite it, but the "Man of God" forbade us from participating, claiming it was spiritually inaccurate. I remember the embarrassment of sitting while everyone else stood—the isolation of being the "odd one out."

But disobedience came at a cost. The discipline in the organization was harsh and unforgettable. Children who broke the rules were subjected to extreme punishment. I witnessed acts that left lasting scars, both physical and emotional. The fear of being singled out, of being punished in front of the congregation, hung over me like a cloud every day.

So when I stayed seated during the Pledge, it wasn't because I didn't believe the words. It wasn't because I didn't love my country or the ideals it stood for. I was just a child trying to survive in two worlds that constantly clashed—one governed by fear, the other by freedom.

And it wasn't just the spiritual rules that set us apart. We weren't allowed to wear name-brand shoes or clothes. The "Man of God" said they were too expensive and that we didn't deserve them. So while other kids wore the latest styles, went on field trips, and attended dances and parties, I watched from the sidelines—wearing off-brand sneakers and carrying the weight of invisible rules.

It was a two-edged sword. At home, I feared the consequences of disobedience. At school, I feared the judgment of my peers. I didn't fit in anywhere. But I kept going. I kept learning. And even in the midst of neglect and fear, something inside me refused to be extinguished.

Two Worlds, One Window

Growing up in the organization, we were taught to avoid anything that resembled competition or reward. Contests were forbidden because they were considered a form of gambling. The "Man of God" had strict views on everything—especially women. If a woman wore pants, she was labeled immoral. Makeup was condemned as a sign of vanity and sin. And if a girl had sex before marriage, she was branded for life.

This rhetoric wasn't just preached—it was expected to be repeated. From the oldest to the youngest, we were encouraged to spread these beliefs to anyone we encountered. It shaped how we saw the world—and how the world saw us.

At school, I stood out. I was different. And kids can be cruel to those who don't fit in. I was teased, laughed at, and picked on. But I wasn't just worried about bullies —I was also afraid of punishment at home. The fear of being beaten for disobedience hung over me constantly.

Still, some of the kids who teased me back then are friends of mine today. And while bullying is never okay, I recognize now that the school environment had limits.

At Gartha B. Peterson Elementary, the administration didn't tolerate abuse. Principal Raymond J. Harris set the tone. He was firm but fair. He had a wooden paddle he called "Mr. Do Right," used for discipline—but never for ritualized punishment. There's a difference between corporal punishment and abuse, and Mr. Harris understood that.

Despite the teasing, public school was a gift. It gave me something I didn't have at home—structure, support, and a glimpse of the outside world. It helped me develop social skills and confidence. It was the window that eventually gave me the strength to break free.

I've described feeling like I was in a box, looking out at the world. School was that window. It showed me that life could be different.

And I was blessed with extraordinary teachers. Mrs. Baldwin, Mrs. Varner, and Mrs. Whetstone in kindergarten. Mrs. Jordan in first grade. Mrs. Kilpatrick and Mrs. Short—who taught us Spanish—in second. Mrs. Ricks in third. Mrs. Davenport in fourth. Mrs. Coleman in fifth. Mrs. Tyson and Mrs. Hastings in sixth. Mrs. Montgomery in seventh.

Their names, faces, and voices are still fresh in my mind, even after more than forty years. Some have passed on, and some are still with us. But they all left a mark.

Mr. Harris wasn't just our principal—he was also the

basketball coach. I wasn't a great player, but he let me join the team anyway. He cared more about character and self-esteem than winning. Our school colors were purple and gold, just like the Lakers. We wanted to wear purple and gold Converse, like Magic Johnson. But I knew I wouldn't be getting those shoes. I didn't even ask. Name-brand shoes were forbidden by the "Man of God." He said they were too expensive and that we didn't deserve them.

That decision ended my short-lived basketball career. But it didn't end my growth. Because even in those moments of disappointment, school gave me something that home never could—hope.

The Shoes I Never Wore

There was a woman in the congregation who lived in Perry Homes Projects, just like my mother. She had three sons, and one of them was a gifted athlete. Wanting to support him, she allowed him to buy a pair of name-brand shoes—something rare and special in our community.

But when the "Man of God" found out, he was furious. He ordered her to burn the shoes. That moment stuck with me—not just because of the shoes, but because of what they represented: pride, individuality, and a mother's love.

I remember wanting to play basketball for Mr. Harris. He would have let me play without the shoes, because he cared more about character than gear. But I didn't want to be the odd one out. So I quietly stepped away from the team.

On game day, I watched my classmates walk into the room wearing their new purple and gold Converse—just like the Lakers. They looked confident, proud, like they belonged. I felt a deep envy. Not just for the shoes, but for the life they seemed to have. A life that felt better than mine. A life that didn't come with so many rules.

In that moment, I didn't feel like I was less talented. I felt like I was less worthy. And that feeling stayed with me far longer than any basketball game ever could.

For years, I measured my value by how well I followed the rules—not the rules of society, or even of faith, but the rules of one man. The "Man of God" decided what we wore, what we said, how we thought, and even how we saw ourselves. And for a long time, I believed him.

I believed that name-brand shoes made you arrogant. That education was unnecessary. That questioning authority meant you didn't love God. I believed that being different meant being wrong.

But somewhere along the way, cracks began to form in that belief system. They started small—moments of envy, like watching my classmates walk in with their purple and gold Converse. Moments of pride, like hearing my teachers praise my intelligence. Moments of kindness, like a friend who laughed with me instead of at me.

Those cracks let in light.

I began to realize that the world outside the organization wasn't evil—it was expansive. It was full of people who cared, who taught, who listened. People who didn't need to control me to love me.

The Picnic That Gave Me Hope

Every year, Mr. Harris—our principal at Gartha B. Peterson Elementary—hosted a special event for students who scored well on the CAT test. It was called the Principal's Picnic, and I was proud to be invited year after year. I always did well on the test, and those picnics became one of the highlights of my childhood.

The picnic was held at Glen Emerald Park, just a short walk from the school. By the time we arrived, Mr. Harris had everything set up: 55-gallon drums filled with ice and sodas, games ready to play, and a warm, welcoming atmosphere that made every child feel special. He would be standing at the BBQ grill when we arrived, cooking hot dogs and hamburgers for us to enjoy.

There was a lake at the park, and we'd gather around

it to watch the fish or skip rocks across the water. We played, laughed, and roamed freely. I remember reaching into those icy barrels and pulling out a cold 12-ounce soda like it was yesterday. That simple joy—cold soda, sunshine, and freedom—was a rare gift.

Even now, decades later, I sometimes return to Glen Emerald Park. I sit under the pavilion, on the same benches we used back then, and let the memories wash over me. Those picnics were more than just celebrations; they were escapes. They were windows into a world where I felt safe, valued, and free.

The world that Mr. Harris and my teachers created for us was a refuge from the stress and fear I lived with at home. As a child, I suffered from daily headaches, and I didn't understand why. Now I know—it was the weight of anxiety, the pressure of living under constant scrutiny and threat.

But school was different. It was a place of encouragement, kindness, and growth. A couple of years ago, we had an elementary school reunion, and seeing Mr. Harris, Mrs. Tyson, Mrs. Coleman (now Mrs. Grant), Mrs. Short, and Mrs. Varner felt like meeting celebrities. I was starstruck. I was grateful.

These educators were more than teachers—they were lifelines. They were instruments God used to give me hope. And I will carry that gratitude with me for the rest of my life.

The Day I Learned to Stand My Ground

Peterson Elementary had a unique rhythm. Some parts felt like a private school—structured, nurturing, and full of dedicated teachers. Other parts felt undeniably "hood"—rough around the edges, full of real-life lessons that tested your spirit. But in the long run, I believe both sides shaped me for the better.

I remember one day, riding the bus home in fifth or sixth grade. I was sitting quietly, feet tucked inside my seat area, when an older kid came down the aisle. Somehow, his foot ended up in my space and he tripped. He immediately got angry and confronted me, acting like it was my fault. I apologized, hoping to defuse the situation.

He went back to his seat at the rear of the bus—but not for long. Moments later, he walked back up, holding a toy gun, and struck me with it. That was it. We started fighting.

We both got in trouble, and the school contacted our parents. When my mother found out, she was furious with me for fighting. I tried to explain—he hit me first, and I wasn't going to let that slide. But she said she was going to report me to the "Man of God" and request that I be punished.

Surprisingly, he took my side. He told my mother he didn't blame me. He said that if you let someone get away with hitting you with a toy gun, next time it might be a real one.

And he was right.

The very next day, I got on the bus and saw the same kid. He called my name, pulled out a real gun, and told me next time he'd use it. I looked him in the eye and said, "Then we'll be fighting all over again." I didn't care that he was older—I wasn't going to be intimidated.

That moment taught me something I carry to this day: bullies often back down when you stand up. I went to school with that same kid for years afterward, and he never bothered me again.

Public school taught me more than academics—it taught me how to navigate conflict, how to read people, and how to protect my dignity. And now, as an adult, if I feel someone is trying to bully me, it's only a matter of time before I confront them. I don't care who they are or what position they hold.

I will not be bullied.

More Hope – Uncle Jesse

My biological father returned from the Air Force with a significant drug addiction. My mother told me he was hooked on heroin. She believed he developed the habit while stationed in Thailand during the Vietnam War.

But I later heard another version of his story from a

family member I reconnected with years later. He told me that my dad had been married before he met my mother. He and his first wife had a nice house, nice cars, and what seemed like a good relationship. Then one day, she told him she no longer wanted to be with him—she wanted to be with another woman.

My dad was devastated. He pleaded with her to stay, but she was unrelenting. According to that family member, that heartbreak might have been what pushed him toward drugs.

I don't know which version is true. What I do know is that my father had an extensive criminal record. He was in and out of prison for years, mostly for petty crimes—stealing to support his addiction.

The "Man of God" constantly berated my father, calling him a "dirty prison nigger" who had abandoned his children. He made sure we knew that if we ever left his teachings, we would end up just like our "nigger daddy."

For years, that image of my father was all I knew—fed to me by the "Man of God" and by my mother. I was told he was a criminal, an addict, a man who didn't care about us. The message was clear: if I ever left the church, I would become him.

I internalized that fear. I made a vow to God that no matter how many children I had, they would always know who their father was. I believed staying in the church was the only way to avoid becoming a failure. I believed my family outside the church were low-lives, and I wanted nothing to do with them.

Then one day, everything changed.

There was a knock at the door. A man stood on our porch with his wife and two daughters. I didn't know who they were, but I could tell by my mother's reaction that she did. She wasn't defensive. She wasn't afraid. She welcomed them.

The man was well-dressed. His family was polished and poised. They looked like prosperity. My mother introduced him:

"This is your uncle, Jesse Mc'Koy. He's your dad's brother."

Uncle Jesse had started working for the post office at seventeen. Later, he was drafted into the Army during the Vietnam War, though he served his tour in Korea. After being honorably discharged, he returned to his government job, where his military service counted toward his retirement. Determined to advance, he earned a bachelor's degree from Georgia State University while working full-time and eventually became a Postal Inspector. He retired with honor and success.

He and his family lived in Texas but were visiting my grandmother, Ms. Martha Shockley. She had asked him to check on us—her son's children. Uncle Jesse asked my mother if he could take us to visit her, and to my surprise, she agreed.

We drove to my grandmother's house, where we met my Aunt Rachel and her son, Johnathan. Aunt Rachel worked at JCPenney. They looked great. They were doing well. They were nothing like the people I had been taught to fear.

Uncle Jesse took us shopping at the mall and told us to get whatever we wanted. I picked out a pair of tennis shoes and a nice pair of blue jeans. I wasn't used to that kind of generosity. It felt awkward—but it also felt good.

That day left a mark on me. It challenged everything I had been taught about my family. I had been told that anyone outside the church was a failure, a drug addict, or a person who didn't care about us. But here was my uncle, arriving in a brand-new Cadillac, looking for his niece and nephews, not to judge us, but to love us.

That day planted a seed. A quiet question bloomed in my mind: What if they were wrong? What if love existed outside the walls of the church?

That ray of hope would grow. And one day, it would help light the path out.

CHAPTER 7
MY TEENAGE YEARS

Hollywood Courts

When I was thirteen, I got my first Summer job through a program called PIC. I was assigned to work in Hollywood Courts, a housing project in Atlanta known for its heavy drug activity. My hours were 8 a.m. to noon, Monday through Friday. My job was simple: pick up trash around the apartments.

Hollywood Courts was unlike anything I had ever seen. The drug traffic was so intense that the police had installed a wrought-iron cage around the entire perimeter of the complex: an attempt to trap dealers during raids. It felt like I was working inside a fortress.

After a few weeks, the local dealers began to recognize me. I was out there every day, picking up trash and minding my business. One day, a few of them approached me with an offer: one hundred dollars a day to be a lookout. All I had to do was yell "Five-O" when I saw the police coming.

It was tempting. A hundred dollars a day was a fortune to a thirteen-year-old. But I turned it down. The five dollars an hour I was making felt like enough, and honestly, I was too scared to get involved. I knew that once you stepped into that world, it was hard to step back out.

Then one day, something happened that I'll never forget.

I was walking through the apartments, picking up trash like usual, when I stumbled upon a confrontation. One of the known drug dealers was holding a gun to a woman's face, accusing her of stealing a bag of drugs. She denied it, pleading with him to believe her.

Suddenly, a man stepped between them—her boyfriend, I later learned. He stood between the barrel of the gun and the woman, begging the dealer not to shoot. The dealer warned him to move or risk being killed, too. But the man didn't budge.

I should have walked away. I should have found safety. But I couldn't. I was frozen—part fear, part curiosity. I watched as the man confessed that his girlfriend had stolen the drugs. He promised to convince her to return them.

The dealer gave him one chance.

"If you don't bring me those drugs, I'm killing both of you," he said.

Minutes later, the man returned with a large bag of crack cocaine. The woman had hidden it under a rock in the woods nearby. I waited, wondering if the dealer would still carry out his threat. But he didn't. He took the drugs, warned them never to cross him again, and walked away.

He spared their lives.

What stayed with me wasn't just the danger—it was the courage. That man stood between a gun and the woman he loved. He risked everything to protect her. At thirteen, that kind of bravery was hard to comprehend. But I admired it deeply.

I finished my summer term at Hollywood Courts.

But I never wanted to go back.

Lessons in the Shadows

After that summer at Hollywood Courts, something shifted in me. I had seen too much—too much danger, too much desperation, too much courage. That one moment, watching a man stand between a gun and the woman he loved, left a mark on me. It taught me that bravery doesn't always come with a badge or a pulpit.

Sometimes, it comes from love. Sometimes, it comes from survival.

I returned to my regular life, but I wasn't the same. The world outside the church had shown me something real, something raw. And it made me start asking questions.

Why did the "Man of God" say that everyone outside his teachings was lost, broken, and evil? Why did he preach that the world was full of nothing but dope heads and criminals, when I had just seen a man risk his life for someone he cared about?

I began to realize that the world wasn't as black and white as I'd been taught. There was pain, yes, but there was also strength. There was chaos, but there was also compassion. And most importantly, there was choice.

That summer taught me that I had choices too.

I didn't have to accept fear as my foundation. I didn't have to believe that leaving the church meant becoming a failure. I didn't have to carry the shame that had been handed to me since childhood.

I could choose to think for myself. I could choose to protect my dignity. I could choose to build a life that honored truth, not control.

It would take time. It would take courage.

But the journey had begun.

The Car, the House, and the Heart Behind It All

At thirteen years old, I started saving up to buy my first car. I didn't have a bank account, but I had someone I trusted—the same elderly woman who once used a borrowed Tupperware bowl to convince my mother to attend a Bible study led by the "Man of God." I asked her to help me save my money, and she agreed—with one condition: once I gave her the money, I'd better have a good reason to ask for it back.

Giving her my money was like putting it in Fort Knox. She was firm, but fair. Week after week, I handed over my earnings, and by the time I was fifteen, I had saved $615. I was well on my way to buying my first car.

Then one night during Bible study, the "Man of God" announced that his cousin had found a brick house for sale—just $5,000. It was a rare deal. He wanted to buy it for the same elderly woman who had been helping me save. She still lived in the projects, while my mother had moved out after marrying a hardworking man who had polio in one leg but never let it slow him down. He worked full-time at the Greyhound Bus Station and did mechanic work on the side. I admired him deeply, He rescued us from Perry Homes Projects and now we lived in a home of our own.

I liked this woman a lot, and even as a teenager, I

saw how meaningful it would be for her to own a home. So when the "Man of God" asked the congregation to raise $5,000, I raised my hand. He called on me, and I pledged $600—nearly everything I had.

By the end of the night, we had raised over $6,000. The house was purchased, and I had just $15 left. But I felt proud. I had helped someone escape the projects.

The house needed serious renovation, and I was there every chance I got. We installed sheetrock, laid tile, repaired plumbing, and poured concrete for a new driveway. We worked late into the night, and through those projects, I learned many of the job skills I still use today. That house turned out beautifully, and her family still lives there to this day.

After that, the woman continued to help me save money. The next year, I saved over $1,000 and bought my first car—a 1970 Ford Maverick. It needed a paint job, and I didn't have enough for insurance. That's when a couple from the church stepped in. They didn't have children of their own, but they were generous beyond measure. They gave me the money I needed for insurance and helped pay for the paint job.

They asked not to be named in my book, and I'll honor that. But anyone who was part of the "Man of God's" organization knows exactly who I'm talking about. Their generosity touched nearly every member —directly or indirectly. They were quiet pillars of support in a place that didn't always offer kindness freely.

This chapter of my life taught me that even in the midst of control and fear, there were people who cared. People who gave. People who helped me believe in something better.

The elderly woman we bought the house for passed away a few years back. She was well over eighty when she died—a sweet, funny, and intelligent lady. She taught me how to better understand people and their behaviors. She used to tell me, "Michael, some people ain't gon' ever sing a song, and they ain't gon' like yours if you sing one." In other words, some people can't be pleased, so don't waste your time trying.

She was a talented seamstress and made many garments for the church members. She was the oldest mother in the church, and I miss her very much.

The Shift in Spirit

As I reflect on the acts of kindness I experienced growing up—the old lady who helped me save money, the congregation that rallied to buy her a home, the generous couple who helped me insure and paint my first car—I realize something deeper. These moments weren't just about generosity. They were glimpses of what the church could have been. What it might have been once.

Even the "Man of God," for all his control and manipulation, had moments that made me wonder if he started out with good intentions. When he encouraged the congregation to raise money for that house, when he gave the first donation himself, when he supported my decision to help—those weren't the actions of a man void of compassion. They were the actions of someone who, at least at one point, believed in community.

But somewhere along the way, something shifted.

The desire to lead became a need to dominate.

The call to guide became a hunger to control.

The spiritual authority he once claimed became a tool for silence, shame, and isolation.

What may have started as a mission to uplift the broken turned into a system that broke the very people it claimed to save.

I've come to believe that the "Man of God" didn't begin as a tyrant. He began as a man with a vision—perhaps even a sincere one. But power is seductive, and unchecked authority has a way of warping even the noblest intentions.

The acts of kindness I witnessed—especially from those who had no obligation to help—taught me that goodness doesn't require control. That love doesn't demand loyalty. That real leadership lifts people up, not holds them down.

Those lessons helped me see the difference between influence and manipulation, between guidance and domination, between faith and fear.

They helped me understand that I didn't have to reject God to reject the "Man of God." That I could walk away from the organization without walking away from hope, or truth, or love.

And that realization was the beginning of freedom.

PART III
THE COST OF FAITH

CHAPTER 8
MARRIAGE AND MANIPULATION

When Shock Became Doctrine

As a teenager, I noticed that one of the "Man of God's" favorite topics was sex. He spoke about it often—especially to young men like me. But his approach wasn't educational or respectful. He didn't use scientific terms or offer guidance rooted in dignity or care. Instead, he used raw, street-level slang—the kind you'd hear on the corners of the roughest neighborhoods.

His language was intentionally crude, designed to shock and provoke. I think he believed that being vulgar made him more relatable, more powerful. And I'll admit—he knew how to get your attention.

He preached that sexual desire was natural, but only acceptable within marriage. He framed masculinity in narrow, aggressive terms, telling us that if we didn't crave sex, we were weak or defective. The pressure to conform to his version of manhood was intense. It wasn't just about faith—it was about identity, about belonging.

I remember feeling confused and embarrassed. At that age, my body was changing, and I didn't fully understand what was happening. There were days I couldn't even get off the school bus because I was too ashamed of what I was experiencing physically. Instead of helping us navigate those changes with compassion, the "Man of God" used them to reinforce his control.

Looking back, I see how damaging that environment was. It didn't teach us respect, emotional maturity, or how to build healthy relationships. It taught us fear, shame, and a distorted view of ourselves and others.

The Marriage That Wasn't Mine to Choose

At eighteen, I believed I was ready to marry. The "Man of God" pointed me toward a girl in the congregation—just fifteen years old. She was beautiful, loyal to the teachings, and already had my attention long before he made the suggestion. Her father was the first recruit of the "Man of God" and had helped him start the organization. That connection made her seem even more ideal in the eyes of the church.

I was infatuated. But there was one problem—she didn't want to marry me.

She made it clear to both the "Man of God" and her father that she wasn't ready. She liked me, she said, and wouldn't mind getting to know me—but she wasn't ready to be a wife. I was crushed. I even cried over the rejection. But for reasons I didn't understand at the time, the "Man of God" and her father were determined to make the marriage happen.

In front of the entire congregation, the "Man of God" confronted her and demanded she explain her refusal. She stood her ground. She spoke honestly, saying she wanted to wait. Looking back, I admire her courage. Few people dared to speak their truth in conflict with him.

But her honesty came at a cost.

She was publicly shamed, chastised, and accused of having immoral intentions. The pressure intensified. Her father threatened to put her out of the house if she didn't agree to marry me. Eventually, she relented—not because she changed her mind, but because she was forced.

I was too young, too naïve, and too trusting of the men I believed were wiser than I. I mistook infatuation for destiny. I even remembered a dream I had as a child where I saw her as my future wife. Maybe it was God's plan, I thought. Or maybe it was just the weight of expectation.

Around that time, I got a phone call from my biological father. Somehow, he had heard I was about to get married. He tried to talk me out of it. But I didn't trust him. After eighteen years of absence, this was only his second attempt to reach out. In my mind, he was a symbol of failure—a man who had abandoned his children. I saw his advice as an attack on my blessing, a distraction from what I believed was divine direction.

He asked me if I had any other options. I told him I did—and that I could choose to avoid responsibility the way he had. His words didn't change my mind.

Looking back, I see how much pressure I was under. I see how little choice I really had. And I see how trust, when placed in the wrong hands, can lead us down paths we were never meant to walk.

I couldn't wait to tell the "Man of God" and the congregation how I had put my dad in his place for trying to block my blessing. I had a testimony! When I shared it, the "Man of God" nodded in approval, and the congregation erupted in loud, congratulatory "Amens," celebrating what they believed was my faithfulness.

At this time, I was a senior in high school with about a month left before graduation. The "Man of God" suggested that I wait until after I graduated to get married so I could find a job first.

Throughout my four years of high school, I had received little to no attention from the girls at school.

But for some reason, once I got engaged, that suddenly changed. Suddenly, several beautiful girls seemed interested in me. Still, I took my new engagement seriously and stayed faithful to my intended.

I couldn't help but wonder—why now? Why did my options suddenly grow once I was no longer available? Maybe it was my height, six feet three inches, or the fact that my appearance had improved over time. Maybe having my own car helped, too. But in my mind, I believed it was something deeper, maybe even spiritual. I convinced myself it was a test, an obstacle meant to hinder the blessing of my marriage. And I was determined not to let anything—or anyone—block me from what I believed was God's plan.

There was a man in the "Man of God's" congregation named Brother James Smith. He was a self-employed landscaper who had learned the trade from the "Man of God" when he was a teenager. Brother Smith worked mainly in the Toco Hills area of Atlanta—a middle-class to upper-class neighborhood, home mostly to Caucasian and Jewish families.

When I was about fourteen, Brother Smith would let me ride the MARTA bus out to Toco Hills every day after school to help him pull weeds and cut grass. The work gave me a little money in my pocket and, more importantly, taught me the value of hard work.

Eventually, Brother Smith gave up self-employment

and took a job with the City of Decatur in the Grounds Maintenance Department. The city had a summer work program for high school students, hiring only about five teenagers each year to work until school resumed. Brother Smith used his influence to help a few of us from the congregation—including me—get those jobs.

Grounds Maintenance was just a fancy way of saying we cut grass and used weed wackers. But I didn't mind. I enjoyed the work, and I was proud of the effort I put in. Every summer from the age of sixteen, I worked for the City of Decatur, and my supervisors always spoke highly of my work ethic. By the time graduation approached, I felt confident they would hire me on a permanent basis.

In June of 1992, I graduated from Alonzo A. Crim Comprehensive High School in Atlanta, Georgia. It was a year that felt heavy with tension and change. That same year, the world watched as Rodney King was brutally beaten by police officers from the LAPD in Los Angeles, California. The attack was caught on video—four white officers violently assaulting an unarmed Black man—and the footage spread across every major news outlet, both national and international.

The beating ignited outrage across the country. The anger and pain of the Black community reached a boiling point, erupting not only in Los Angeles but in cities all over America, including my own—Atlanta. I remember sitting in class as a senior, listening to my classmates talk about going downtown to join the riots. It was surreal to think that something happening on the other side of the country could spark so much fire right where we were.

I felt that same anger. The same frustration. But I was also afraid. Unlike many of my classmates, I knew if I got caught doing something like that, my mother would still give me a whooping, even at eighteen. So I stayed put.

Some of my classmates didn't. They skipped school, went downtown, and came back bragging about what they'd done—looting stores, vandalizing buildings, even attacking white people. One classmate told us how he jumped on top of a car and kicked in the windshield while a white driver sat inside. The pride in his voice was chilling, but I understood where the rage came from. We were all angry.

What made it worse was the trial that followed. Despite the clear video evidence showing Rodney King being beaten without mercy, the white officers were all acquitted. The jury found them not guilty. Once again, the justice system had protected the guilty and betrayed the truth.

Black people everywhere were outraged. It felt like a wound had been reopened, one we had never been allowed to heal. Still, there was nothing we could do about it. The message was clear, and it echoed the infamous line from New Jack City, when Nino Brown said, "Don't get mad, Black people—it's the law."

In 1994, O.J. Simpson was accused of murdering Nicole Brown Simpson and Ron Goldman. The evidence against him was overwhelming—so much so that most Black people, including myself, believed he was guilty. But the truth didn't matter as much as what the moment represented. Because O.J. was Black, we wanted him to win. We wanted him to use his fame, his money, and his "dream team" of lawyers to beat the same system that white folks had used against us for centuries. We wanted payback for all the times justice had been denied to us.

And Johnny Cochran gave us exactly that—**with style.**

O.J. suffered from arthritis, no doubt a byproduct of his years as a professional running back in the NFL. His condition caused his hands to swell whenever he didn't take his medication. During the trial, one of the gloves found at the murder scene was introduced as key evidence. The prosecution decided to have O.J. try it on in front of the jury to prove that it belonged to him.

But Johnny Cochran was smarter than that. He instructed O.J. not to take his arthritis medication before the demonstration, so when O.J. tried on the glove in court, it didn't fit. That moment changed everything. Cochran stood before the jury and delivered what became one of the most iconic lines in courtroom history:

"If it doesn't fit, you must acquit."

After only about three hours of deliberation, the jury returned a verdict of **Not Guilty.**

Black folks across the country were ecstatic—including me. To us, it felt like payback for Rodney King. I knew in my heart that O.J. was probably guilty, but I saw it as a kind of poetic justice. The same way thousands of white lynch mobs had murdered innocent Black people throughout history and walked free, O.J. walked free that day.

If justice had been done for Rodney King, O.J. Simpson might have been found guilty for Nicole Brown Simpson and Ron Goldman. Every time I see their families—Ron Goldman's father or Nicole Brown's loved ones—I feel a deep sadness. Their pain was real. Their loss became a sacrifice, a tragic outlet for the collective outrage that the Black community carried after Rodney King.

The O.J. trial took place in 1994, but let me step back for a moment—to 1992.

It was a miracle that I even earned enough credits to graduate. I went to school when I wanted to, showed up late most days, and did just enough to get by. Looking back now, that sounds tragic. I had the ability to learn, but no ambition to make the most of it.

Still, by the grace of God, I graduated from Alonzo A. Crim Comprehensive High School at the Atlanta Civic Center with the rest of my class. That day was unforgettable. It's amazing how strong the bond is between high school classmates—some of them I had known since kindergarten. They become part of your story forever, some more deeply than others.

It's been over 30 years since that day, and I still remember the song we sang at graduation—a special rendition of "It's So Hard to Say Goodbye to Yesterday" by Boyz II Men. Our version went: "It's so hard to say goodbye to Crim High."

It might sound corny to anyone else, but to me—and to the other ninety or so graduates of the Class of 1992—it was a beautiful, emotional tribute. And even now, we still think about that song, and that moment, with a smile.

Shandon Anderson was one of my graduating classmates. I first met Shandon in the fall of 1989, when we both arrived at Crim High School as freshmen. I had already heard of him and his great potential as a basketball player, but I hadn't yet seen him play. Before I ever witnessed his basketball talent, I shared a Geometry class with him. I was impressed by how intelligent he was and how quickly he grasped new concepts. He was an exceptionally good student, and I admired the way he carried himself off the court. Shandon dressed more like a college student than a high schooler. Looking back, I can see that Shandon didn't dress according to where he was—he dressed for where he was going.

Shandon had an older brother, Willie Anderson, who had played in the NBA for the San Antonio Spurs. Before I saw Shandon play, I doubted whether he was good enough to make it to the professional level. I thought that if he did, it would only be because of his brother's influence, since Willie had an impressive career alongside David Robinson. But once I saw Shandon play for myself, I understood what all the hype was about. He had all the physical tools of a prototypical NBA guard—he stood 6'6", was strong and athletic, and moved on the court with a combination of grace and power. He was an excellent finisher at the basket, and it was clear that he had what it took to reach the next level.

Although we weren't close friends, we developed a mutual respect and camaraderie throughout our high school years. Shandon went on to play college basketball at the University of Georgia, where his team made it to the Sweet Sixteen during his senior year. He later entered the NBA draft and was selected by the Utah Jazz, reaching the NBA Finals two years in a row alongside Karl Malone, John Stockton, and Bryon Russell. They might have won the championship—if it weren't for that guy named Michael Jordan and the Chicago Bulls. Shandon was later traded to the New York Knicks and eventually to the Miami Heat, where he won an NBA championship with Dwyane Wade, Shaquille O'Neal, and Alonzo Mourning.

My high school graduation was one of the best days of my life. The Man of God and his wife even allowed me to use their Cadillac to drive to and from the ceremony. As I write about it now, I realize why this memory stands out so strongly in my mind—it was one of the last meaningful moments of my youth before I got married three months later.

I graduated in June of 1992, and I was married on September 1, 1992. I was 18 years old, and my fiancée was 15. In Georgia, where we lived, the minimum age to marry was 16 with parental consent. But the Man of God was very "anti-establishment." He believed the rules didn't apply to him—a mindset that came from his narcissistic personality. That defiant attitude contributed to the power he held over his congregation. We saw him as a man unafraid to challenge the system.

When it came to arranging marriages for underage couples—which was illegal in Georgia—he would always find a way around it. Since my fiancée was only 15, he came up with a plan for us to go to Alabama, where the minimum marriage age was 14 with parental consent. The Man of God persuaded both sets of parents —hers and mine—to travel with us to Anniston,

Alabama, where we were married at the courthouse before a Justice of the Peace.

We weren't the first young couple he arranged to marry that way, and we wouldn't be the last. Some girls were as young as 14, married off to men in their twenties. They'll have to tell their own stories one day, and from what I've heard, those stories are harrowing. The Man of God even wanted to arrange marriages for girls as young as 13, but he couldn't find a state that would allow it.

Since I was 18, I didn't need parental consent, but my wife's parents signed off for her to marry at 15. And just like that, I went from being a high school kid to a married man, responsible for a wife and a life I was far from ready for.

At the time we were married, I was working for the City of Decatur. It was only a summer job, but it felt good to be earning money and taking care of myself and my new wife. It was 1992—the same year Bill Clinton defeated George H. W. Bush for the presidency of the United States. I remember the Clinton campaign running that one commercial over and over, quoting Bush saying, "Read my lips, no new taxes!" That promise helped him win the previous election. The only problem was, he went back on his word a couple of years into his presidency and raised taxes anyway. The American people felt betrayed.

I even remember Bill Clinton coming to Decatur, Georgia, where I worked, to give a campaign speech at Decatur High School during the summer of 1991. Clinton was young, handsome, and charismatic. George Bush didn't stand a chance. It's a shame, really, because Bush seemed to be a capable leader. In many ways, I think the country might have benefited if he'd been given a second term.

I enjoyed working for the City of Decatur in the Grounds Maintenance Department. It gave me a sense of responsibility, and I was proud to be providing for my wife. I was also looking forward to consummating our marriage. We were taught that using birth control was a sin and that the Bible said to "be fruitful and multiply." Most religious people interpret that as having as many children as possible, but I've come to see it differently. I believe the scripture means to be fruitful first, then multiply. If you're not a fruitful person—if you're not stable, mature, or ready for the responsibility—you have no business multiplying. That's how I see it now.

The Man of God and his wife allowed my new bride and me to live with them when we were first married. They had an extra room in their house, and we accepted their offer. We had both experimented with sex before, but not enough to lose the title of virgin. Before our wedding night, the Man of God pulled me aside and advised me to use plenty of Vaseline before being intimate with my wife. He even gave me my first jar of it.

We were both inexperienced and didn't really know what we were doing, but I followed his advice as best I could. Somehow, we managed a successful consummation. We actually had good sexual chemistry, but good sex alone isn't enough to make a marriage work. At first, I was the one initiating intimacy, but it wasn't long before she began initiating as well. Apparently, she enjoyed it just as much as I did, well, maybe not as much as I did, but she enjoyed it too.

The next day, we decided to take a short honeymoon road trip. I took a couple of days off from work, and we hit the road in my red 1970 Ford Maverick. That was my second car. My first had also been a 1970 Ford Maverick —black with no pinstripes. I bought it when I was fifteen, just two weeks before my sixteenth birthday. I remember how eager I was to take my driver's license test. I had worked hard to save up enough money for that car, but unfortunately, I didn't have it long before I wrecked it.

It happened on a Saturday. We were working on an old house we'd bought, painting and cleaning. I had been using a cleaning agent called mineral spirits—a strong chemical that smells like gasoline and is used to clean oil-based paint. Anyone who's worked with oil-based paint knows how difficult it is to wash off, and that tells you just how strong mineral spirits are. The fumes can make you feel lightheaded, almost like you're high. After working with it all day, I wasn't thinking clearly. I decided to drive home, which turned out to be a terrible decision.

On the way, a car stopped suddenly in front of me. By the time I hit the brakes—BAM!—it was too late. I hit that car so hard it nearly tore the hood off mine. That accident ended my first car, but I was resourceful. I saved up and bought another one shortly before getting married. It was the same make and model, but I had it painted cherry red with white pinstripes on the sides. It was a beautiful car.

We drove it to Chickamauga Lake in Tennessee for our honeymoon. It was a familiar place for both of us—we'd gone there as kids—but this time, it felt different. It was our first time there as husband and wife. The park felt more peaceful, the sand on the beach looked whiter, and the lake seemed to sparkle more than I remembered. That's what happens when you're there with someone you're deeply infatuated with.

I was completely taken with her. To me, what I felt was love—real love—and over time it only grew stronger. But that love was never truly reciprocated. She was my heart, but I never felt that same depth of feeling coming back from her.

We traveled from Tennessee to Cherokee, North

Carolina, to the Indian Reservation—another place we both knew well. We spent the night there. That night was the first time my new wife initiated intimacy with me. It caught me by surprise, because I had always believed that it was the man's role to initiate sex.

I still remember that moment clearly. In the middle of the night, she woke me gently with soft kisses, and before long, she took the lead. It was the first time I'd ever experienced something like that, and it left a lasting impression on me.

The next day, we headed back home to Atlanta. It was an enjoyable trip for me, and I believe she enjoyed it too. But looking back now—with more life experience and understanding—I see things differently. How could I have expected my wife to truly enjoy a marriage she was forced into, with a man she only kind of liked?

At fifteen, most girls are thinking about finishing high school, planning for college, or dreaming about their future careers. But this young girl was thrust into a marriage and preparing to become a mother, with a man who wasn't even her choice. She was as much a victim in this as I was, if not more.

Living the Life I Thought I Wanted

After the wedding, I expected things to feel complete. I thought marriage would bring peace, purpose, and maybe even joy. I had followed the path laid out for me by the "Man of God," trusted the judgment of elders, and fulfilled what I believed was a divine calling. But almost immediately, I realized that what I had entered wasn't a union; it was a contract signed under pressure.

We were two teenagers trying to play the roles of husband and wife, but the foundation was cracked from the start. She hadn't chosen me freely, and deep down, I knew it. I tried to be a good husband. I tried to love her the way I thought I was supposed to. But love cannot grow where fear and obligation have taken root.

There were moments of connection—brief flashes where we laughed, talked, or shared something real—but they were rare. Most of the time, I felt like I was chasing something that didn't want to be caught. I was trying to build a life with someone who had been forced to stand beside me. And she was trying to survive in a world that had denied her voice.

I didn't have the emotional tools to understand what was happening. I was young, inexperienced, and still under the influence of a system that valued obedience over introspection. I thought that if I just worked harder, prayed more, and followed the rules more strictly, things would get better. But they didn't.

We were both hurting, and neither of us had the freedom to say it out loud. Looking back, I see how much pressure we were under; not just from each other, but from the entire congregation. Our marriage had become a symbol of loyalty, submission, and spiritual alignment. To admit that it wasn't working would have been seen as rebellion.

So we stayed silent. We stayed together. We tried to make it work. But silence has a weight. Over time, it began to crush the parts of me that still believed in love, in choice, in freedom.

Used Against Me

After the wedding, I tried to settle into the role of husband. I wanted to believe I had made the right decision. I wanted to believe that love would grow, that trust would follow, and that obedience would be rewarded. But the truth was harder to face.

My wife hadn't chosen me freely, and the "Man of God" never let me forget it.

Whenever it suited him—whether during a sermon, a private conversation, or a moment of public humiliation—he would remind me that she hadn't wanted to marry me. He used it as a weapon, a way to remind me of my weakness and keep me in line.

He would say things like, "You had to beg for a wife. She didn't even want you," or, "If it wasn't for me, Bronny would have never married you."

It didn't matter that he had orchestrated the

marriage. It didn't matter that her father had threatened her. It didn't matter that I was just a young man trying to follow what I thought was divine guidance. He twisted the narrative to serve his control.

And I believed him.

I carried that shame with me. I questioned my worth. I wondered if I was truly lovable, or if companionship had only been granted to me as a form of spiritual charity. I tried harder. I prayed more. I stayed silent.

But deep down, I knew something was wrong.

The same man who had pushed us together was now using our pain to keep us bound. He turned our story into a cautionary tale, one that kept me humble, obedient, and afraid.

Looking back, I see it clearly now. It wasn't about love. It wasn't about guidance. It was about power. And the more I doubted myself, the more control he had.

Yet even in that darkness, something inside me began to stir; a quiet voice, a flicker of truth, a question I couldn't ignore: *What if this isn't what God intended? What if love isn't supposed to feel like this?*

Microwaves and Misunderstandings

After living with the "Man of God" and his wife for a couple of months, my wife and I moved into an apartment with another newlywed couple from the congregation. They were a little older than us, and for the most part, we got along well. We shared the space, the responsibilities, and even the kitchen.

One day, they bought a microwave. It was a luxury we couldn't afford at the time, so I was grateful to be able to use it. I made sure to treat it with care. But soon, they began to complain that we weren't closing "the door" after using it.

I assumed they meant the microwave door. So I told my wife, "Let's make sure we close it every time." And we did. I thought that was the end of it.

Then one day, I came home from work, and the microwave was gone.

I asked my wife what happened. She told me our roommates had taken it away because we weren't closing the door like they'd asked. I was confused—we had been closing the microwave door every time. She agreed.

So I went to talk to our roommate. That's when I learned the truth: he wasn't talking about the microwave door. He was talking about the front door—the solid wood door to the apartment. We had been leaving it open on hot days to let in some air, though the wrought-iron screen door with double locks was always secured.

He wanted both doors closed at all times.

I was stunned. The entire disagreement had been based on a misunderstanding. I had been thinking about one door, and he had meant another. It was such a simple miscommunication, yet it had turned into a silent standoff.

That day taught me three important lessons:

- **Lesson One:** Misunderstandings can start over the smallest things. Clarity matters.
- **Lesson Two:** People can be petty. Removing a microwave over a door left open—especially when the screen door was locked—felt extreme.
- **Lesson Three:** Sometimes, you have to do what it takes to keep the peace. Even when it seems unnecessary, it's better to bend than to break.

I reassured him that from then on, I'd keep both doors closed. Not because I agreed with his logic, but because I valued harmony more than being right.

Living with others teaches you lessons you don't learn in sermons. It teaches patience, humility, and the art of choosing your battles wisely.

The Weight We Carried

From the outside, we looked like a young couple fulfilling a divine calling. Inside, we were two teenagers trying to survive a life neither of us had truly chosen.

The emotional toll of our marriage began before the vows were even spoken. My wife had been pressured into saying yes. I had been convinced it was God's will. But beneath the surface, there was pain—hers, mine, and a silence that grew louder with each passing day.

She was distant. Not cruel, not cold—just absent in a way that made me feel invisible. I tried to be patient. I tried to be loving. But I was also confused, frustrated, and deeply insecure. I didn't know how to build intimacy with someone who had been forced to stand beside me.

And the "Man of God" didn't help. He reminded me often—sometimes subtly, sometimes publicly—that she hadn't wanted me. He used her reluctance as a tool to keep me humble, to keep me obedient. It was as if my marriage was a favor he had granted me, and I owed him for it.

That kind of manipulation seeps into everything. It affects how you see yourself, how you communicate, how you love. I began to question my worth—not just as a husband, but as a man. I wondered if I was lovable, or if I was simply being tolerated.

We rarely talked about our feelings. We didn't have the language for it, and we didn't feel safe enough to try. Our home was quiet, but not peaceful. It was filled with unspoken tension, unmet expectations, and the weight of spiritual obligation.

I carried guilt for wanting more. I carried shame for not being enough. And she carried the burden of a life she hadn't asked for.

Looking back, I see how much we both suffered—not because we were bad people, but because we were placed in a situation that denied us choice, voice, and freedom.

Love cannot grow in captivity. And marriage cannot thrive under manipulation.

But even in that pain, I began to learn. I began to feel the stirrings of truth. I began to understand that obedience without understanding is not holiness—it's bondage.

And slowly, I began to ask myself: What would my life look like if I chose it for myself?

CHAPTER 9
FATHERHOOD AND THE BREAKING OF CHAINS

Becoming a Father

After we married, life settled into a rhythm—work, home, and regular attendance at the "Man of God's" teachings. One message he preached often was the importance of a man taking care of his family. He spoke directly to me about how my father had abandoned us, and that message struck a deep chord in my heart.

I vowed I would never do my wife and children the way my father had done me. I believed the "Man of God" was a champion of family life, and that belief drew me in even deeper. I wanted to be the kind of man who stayed. Who showed up. Who loved without condition.

More than anything, I wanted to be a father.

But months passed, and my wife didn't get pregnant.

We were trying—often—but nothing happened. I started to worry. I began to wonder if our marriage wasn't blessed by God. That thought consumed me.

Looking back, I see how flawed my thinking was. Scripture says, "Blessed is the womb that is barren, and the paps that never gave suck." Children are a blessing, yes—but their absence doesn't mean a curse.

Still, I was young, eager, and desperate to prove that I could be the father I never had.

Then, in February of 1993, my wife told me she had missed her cycle. I rushed to the drugstore to buy a pregnancy test. I handed it to her, and she went into the bathroom. I stood outside the door, heart pounding, waiting.

And then—I heard the words I'd been longing for: "It's positive."

She was pregnant. I was going to be a father.

I was ecstatic. For as long as I could remember, I had dreamed of having a son. Someone who looked like me, depended on me, and knew I would never let him down. I was ready to give him everything I never had.

That day, I made a vow to God: no matter how many children He gave me, I would never abandon them. I would be present. I would be faithful. I would be the father I needed growing up.

And I meant it with all my heart.

Cravings and Care

I truly enjoyed taking care of my wife while she was pregnant. Her cravings would hit at all hours—sometimes at two in the morning—and without hesitation, I'd get up and find whatever she wanted. Most nights, it was food from Waffle House or butter pecan ice cream. I'd drive out, pick up her favorites, and often grab a bouquet of flowers while I was at it.

It wasn't just about satisfying cravings. It was about showing her that I saw her, that I appreciated her, and that I understood the sacrifice she was making—carrying our child, enduring the discomfort, and giving her body to bring my heart's desire into the world. I wanted her to feel cherished.

Many women feel that pregnancy makes them less desirable, but to me, nothing could be further from the truth. I thought my wife was more beautiful while she was pregnant. There was a glow about her—a quiet strength, a softness, a radiance I couldn't ignore.

She was giving me a son—a child I had longed for. Every late-night trip, every scoop of ice cream, every bouquet was my way of saying thank you.

It was a season of love expressed through small, sacred gestures, and I wouldn't trade those moments for anything.

Don't Challenge Me

It was July 4, 1993. My wife was six and a half months pregnant, and the "Man of God" had suggested the congregation celebrate the holiday at a nearby park by the lake. That morning, I greeted my wife warmly: "Good morning, sweetheart. How are you today?" But she didn't respond. She stayed silent the entire ride to the meeting site, and I couldn't understand why.

As soon as we arrived, she saw the "Man of God" and ran to greet him with a smile and enthusiasm she hadn't shown me all morning. I was stunned. I had done nothing but treat her like a queen, yet she wouldn't speak to me, but she greeted another man with joy.

So I confronted her. Right there, in front of the "Man of God," I asked, "How is it that you wouldn't speak to me this morning, your husband, but you greet another man so kindly?"

I expected support. I thought the "Man of God" would affirm the biblical principle of marriage—that a wife should cleave to her husband. Instead, he erupted.

"I'm not just another man—I'm the Man of God! I'm above you! You ain't nobody! I don't care if she never speaks to you—she's supposed to speak to me!"

I was stunned but stayed calm. "Doesn't the Bible say a husband and wife should forsake all and cleave to one another?" I asked.

He snapped back, "So now you're trying to be a smart ass."

"No," I said quietly. "I'm just trying to call for my rights as her husband."

That was enough to trigger a hazing campaign against me. My mother, who had long been loyal to the "Man of God," even suggested that the men of the church beat me. Thankfully, that never happened, but the emotional punishment was relentless. The "Man of God" never forgave me for that moment. He brought it up for years, using it as a weapon to shame and isolate me whenever I stepped out of line.

But I didn't mind, because I knew I was right.

The Bible teaches that husband and wife should cleave to one another. Yet in that church, it seemed the real expectation was that husband and wife should cleave to the "Man of God." That realization cut deep; not just because I was dismissed, but because I finally saw how twisted the hierarchy had become.

Still, I felt proud of myself. I had challenged him. And in that place, challenging the "Man of God" was seen as rebellion. He labeled me "high-minded" and "exalted," and that label followed me for years.

But I wore it with quiet pride, because I was one of the few who dared to speak up when something didn't feel right. And deep down, I knew that one day, a major confrontation between us was inevitable.

Elevated, But Not Free

After our confrontation, I expected to be punished—and in many ways, I was. Emotionally, socially, and spiritually, I carried the weight of that moment. The "Man of God" never forgot that I had challenged him. He brought it up often, using it as a reminder of my place.

But then, something unexpected happened.

He began to call on me more.

I was asked to take on leadership roles in the church. I was given responsibilities, visibility, and even a seat on a televised panel sponsored by the House of Prayer. It felt like a promotion, but it was also a paradox.

On one hand, I was honored. I had grown up in this organization, and being trusted with leadership felt like validation. I wanted to believe it meant I was respected—that my voice mattered, that I had earned a place of influence.

But on the other hand, I knew the truth. This wasn't about empowerment; it was about containment. By pulling me closer, the "Man of God" could keep me under watch. He could shape my narrative, control my image, and use my presence to reinforce his own authority.

It was a clever tactic: elevate the challenger, and you neutralize the threat.

I sat on that panel, spoke to the congregation, and

carried out my duties with sincerity. But inside, I wrestled with the contradiction. I was being used to represent a system I was beginning to question. I was speaking on behalf of a man I no longer fully trusted.

And yet, I kept showing up. Because part of me still hoped.

Hoped that I could make a difference.

Hoped that leadership meant change.

Hoped that maybe, just maybe, I could help steer the ship toward something more honest.

But deep down, I knew I wasn't free. I was elevated, yes—but I was still tethered.

Brother Allen had a disturbing habit. He seemed to enjoy robbing men of the respect and affection that rightfully belonged to them—from their wives, their children, their homes. It was as if he treated it like a game, measuring whether he could command more reverence than the actual husband or father. And too often, he succeeded.

It was painful to watch. Even more painful to experience.

Though the "Man of God" rarely opened the Bible during his teachings, I began to read it for myself. And what I found didn't always match what I had been taught. It was the first time I truly challenged him; not just with words, but with scripture, with truth, with conviction.

He hated to be challenged. But he also knew he couldn't just say anything to me and expect blind obedience. That's what separated me from most others in the congregation. I didn't speak up every time I should have, but there was a limit to how far my silence and hypocrisy could go.

I believed in freedom of speech. I believed that every person had the right to speak their truth, even if others disagreed. And I believed that if you were right—truly right—then God was on your side, no matter who stood against you. Even if that opponent was the "Man of God" himself.

That belief gave me strength. It gave me clarity. And it gave me the courage to begin breaking free from the spiritual fog I had lived in for so long.

Truth in the Margins

The "Man of God" often preached about the twelve tribes of Israel, claiming that each tribe contained 12,000 people. He would then declare that 12,000 times 12,000 equals 144,000—and that this was the biblical reason the tribes numbered 144,000.

It may seem like a small thing, but it wasn't. Because 12,000 times 12,000 equals 144 million, not 144,000. The correct calculation is 12 times 12,000, which equals 144,000.

I brought this to his attention privately, thinking I was helping. I wasn't trying to challenge him or prove that I was smarter. I simply wanted the truth to be spoken accurately—especially in front of guests and new members.

But he didn't see it that way.

He accused me of being "high-minded," of trying to challenge his authority. From that point on, he continued to repeat the incorrect math in his sermons. I would sit there, embarrassed, especially when visitors were present. But what could I do?

Another one of his favorite sermons came from Matthew 23:23, where Jesus rebukes the Pharisees for neglecting the weightier matters of the law. The "Man of God" would quote it as, "Ye tithe of mint and succumb."

I wasn't familiar with the verse at first, so I looked it up. The actual scripture reads: "Ye tithe of mint, dill, and cumin, and have neglected the weightier matters of the law."

I did more research and learned that mint, dill, and cumin were valuable spices in biblical times—used for trade, much like currency. But the word succumb wasn't in the verse. It wasn't even close.

Again, I brought this to him privately. And again, he was offended. He called me a "young upstart," accused me of thinking I was smarter than he was, and labeled me "high-minded."

It became clear that he saw himself as the sole interpreter of scripture, as if only he understood the mysteries of the Bible. But the truth was his grasp of scripture, at least in these moments, was flawed. And his refusal to be corrected revealed more than just pride. It revealed fear.

Fear of losing control. Fear of being questioned. Fear of truth.

I wasn't trying to undermine him. I was trying to honor the Word. But in that church, even truth could be seen as rebellion.

The Ripple Effect

At first, my resistance was subtle. I didn't shout or storm out. I simply read the Word for myself, asked questions when something didn't add up, and refused to pretend that everything made sense when it didn't.

But in a place like that, even quiet rebellion echoes.

Some members of the congregation began to watch me with suspicion. They had been conditioned to see any form of questioning as pride, arrogance, or spiritual danger. To them, I was "high-minded," a label the "Man of God" used often to isolate anyone who dared to think independently. Once that label was placed on you, it stuck. It followed you into every room, every conversation, every sermon.

Others, though, responded differently.

There were people who pulled me aside quietly. They didn't say much, but their eyes said everything. A nod. A whispered, "I've wondered that too." A moment of shared silence that felt like solidarity. They were afraid to speak, but they were listening. And they were watching.

Some began to ask their own questions—not publicly, but in private. They wanted to know what I had read, what I had discovered, what I thought. They were hungry for truth but terrified of the consequences.

And then there were those who admired me. Not because I was defiant, but because I was honest. Because I was willing to say what they couldn't. Because I was still showing up, still serving, still loving—while quietly refusing to surrender my mind.

I became a symbol; not of rebellion, but of possibility.

The "Man of God" hated that. He tried to use my visibility to control me, but the more I stood firm, the more others began to see that obedience wasn't the same as righteousness. That loyalty didn't mean silence. That faith could coexist with discernment.

My quiet rebellion didn't shake the walls, but it cracked the foundation. And once the cracks appeared, others began to see through them.

My First Born, Michael Oglesby Jr.

On September 24, 1993, my wife was thirty-eight weeks pregnant and scheduled for a routine check-up. Everything seemed normal until the doctor detected a slight heart murmur in our unborn child. After careful consideration, he recommended inducing labor so the issue could be addressed as soon as possible.

We called the "Man of God" to inform him and ask for guidance. He agreed with the doctor's recommendation, so we gave permission to begin the induction process. My wife was admitted to the hospital and given medication to start labor.

I had already worked a full day and spent more than twelve hours at the hospital. The doctors told me labor wouldn't begin for another twenty-four hours and suggested that I go home to rest. I took their advice, went home, and slept.

The next morning, September 25, 1993, I arrived at the hospital around 8:30 a.m., only to find that my wife had already given birth to our first son. I had missed it.

He weighed four pounds, fifteen ounces. Small, but perfect. We named him **Michael Oglesby Jr.**

When I walked into the delivery room, the first thing my wife said was, "I caught hell." I'll never forget those words. They pierced me. I held her close, overwhelmed with gratitude. She had endured so much to bring our son into the world, and I was forever thankful—to her and to God.

From that moment on, I made a vow: I would never tolerate my children disrespecting their mother. She had suffered for them, sacrificed for them, and she deserved their utmost respect. As her husband and their father, it was my duty to ensure that.

Becoming a father filled me with pride and purpose. I was determined to give my son everything I never received from my own father. His absence had left a deep wound—one that was constantly reopened by the way my mother and the "Man of God" spoke about him. They called him a drug addict, a deadbeat, a failure. I carried that resentment, and I used it as fuel.

I wanted to be different. I wanted to be present.

Still, I was cautious. I didn't want my son to be spoiled. I showed him love and affection, but I was mindful of how often others held him during the long church services. He was a beautiful baby, and everyone wanted to hold him, but I kept track, insisting that he be put down after a while.

Oddly enough, he didn't smile at first. He was quiet, observant. But I was determined to make him smile. I bought a little squeaky monkey toy and would squeeze it in front of his face, talking to him in baby talk—goo goo gi gi—until one day that beautiful smile broke through.

And then came the laugh.

It was the sound of joy. The sound of hope. The sound of a new beginning.

Matthew Oglesby – A Gentle Spirit

Just eleven months after the birth of our first son, my wife and I found ourselves preparing for another blessing. Though doctors advised waiting four to six weeks before resuming intimacy, we usually only made it to five. Needless to say, it wasn't long before she was pregnant again.

On August 22, 1994, I was working for the City of Decatur Street Department when I received an urgent call from my wife—her water had broken. I dropped everything, jumped into my 1970 Ford Maverick, and sped down I-20 West with my heart racing and nerves buzzing. I expected panic when I arrived, but instead, my wife was calm, collected, and already packing her bags. She was even arranging for a babysitter for Michael Jr., who was just eleven months old.

Her poise amazed me. She was a trooper: graceful and grounded. Her calmness helped settle my nerves, and together we made our way to Grady Hospital.

This time, I was determined not to miss the birth. I had arrived too late for Michael Jr.'s delivery, and I wasn't going to let that happen again. I was in the room when our second son was born, and though I didn't feel the physical pain, I felt every contraction in my spirit. I was anxious, overwhelmed, and deeply moved.

My mother was also in the delivery room. She had a gift—a calming, nurturing presence that made her beloved among the women in the congregation. She had been present for the birth of more than one hundred children, including eleven of mine. My wife insisted that she be there, and I wholeheartedly agreed.

Matthew's delivery was smoother, much easier than Michael Jr.'s. He came into the world with a head full of sandy brown hair and a quiet strength. He was beautiful, and I was proud beyond words to now have two sons.

Michael Jr. and Matthew were only eleven months apart. For one month each year, they were technically the same age, and they started elementary school together. I took them to school almost every day, eager to watch them grow and succeed.

Because they were in the same grade, the school placed them in separate classes. But they shared the same lunch period. On the first day of school, Matthew's kindergarten teacher noticed he wasn't eating. His tray sat untouched. She tried to encourage him, even called over other teachers, but he still wouldn't eat.

Finally, someone suggested bringing over his brother.

Michael Jr. walked over and calmly explained, "Matthew won't eat because he hasn't said his blessing."

My wife and I had taught all our children to say a Bible verse or a prayer before eating. So the teachers asked Matthew to say his verse. He bowed his head and said, "Walk not after the flesh, but after the Spirit. Amen." Then he began to eat.

The teachers were touched. From that day forward, they came over every lunch period just to hear Matthew say his verse. They fell in love with both of my boys—not just for their manners, but for the spirit they carried.

Katrina Michelle Oglesby – A Glimpse of Grace

About a year after Matthew was born, my wife discovered she was pregnant again. I assumed we'd be welcoming another boy, and I was excited. All the times I had imagined having children, I never once considered the possibility of having a daughter.

Then came the routine checkup. The doctor looked at us and said, "You're having a girl."

I was stunned. I wasn't ready. I didn't know how to be a father to a girl. I felt lost—and afraid.

The fear wasn't just about the unknown. It was rooted in the stories I had heard growing up in the "Man of God's" congregation. Stories of men accused of violating their daughters. Stories repeated often—sometimes exaggerated, sometimes fabricated—to demonize others. But at the time, I believed them. And those stories planted seeds of doubt and fear in my heart.

I began to question myself. Would I be safe for my daughter? Could I be trusted? Could I change her diaper, bathe her, or kiss her without fear? I had helped with my sons without hesitation, but this felt different. The weight of generational trauma and spiritual manipulation clouded what should have been a moment of pure joy.

Then came a moment of clarity.

One night, around 2:00 a.m., my wife had a craving for a patty melt and hash browns—scattered, smothered, covered, and topped—from Waffle House. I got out of bed without hesitation and drove to get her food. She was carrying our third child, and I wanted her to know I was with her every step of the way.

When I arrived, I noticed a young Black father holding his baby girl in his arms. She was beautiful—chocolate brown skin, afro-style hair, diamond earrings sparkling in the dim light. Watching him cradle her, I felt something shift inside me.

It was peace. It was joy. It was God.

In that moment, I knew I was ready. I knew I would change my daughter's diaper, bathe her, kiss her, and protect her. I knew I would be her father, her teacher, her shield—from her first breath to my last.

On August 16, 1996, Katrina Michelle Oglesby was

born. We named her after my sister, Trina-Cole. And incredibly, she looked just like the baby I had seen in that Waffle House—like God had given me a glimpse of my future, and it was beautiful.

Katrina – Redefining Fatherhood

From the moment Katrina was born, something shifted in me. Holding her in my arms for the first time, I felt a kind of love I hadn't known before. It was different from what I felt with my sons—not stronger or better, but uniquely tender. She was delicate, beautiful, and full of quiet power. And I knew, without question, that I was hers.

In those early days, I bonded with her in ways I never imagined. I changed her diapers, bathed her, kissed her forehead, and whispered prayers over her tiny body. All the fears I'd carried before her birth—about whether I could be trusted, whether I could be gentle, whether I could be safe—were washed away in the rhythm of caring for her.

She needed me. And I needed her.

I found myself watching her sleep, marveling at her tiny fingers, her soft curls, her peaceful breath. I'd sing to her, rock her, and sometimes just sit quietly beside her crib, overwhelmed by both the responsibility and the privilege of being her father.

And through her, I began to understand something deeper about masculinity.

Growing up, I was taught that being a man meant being strong, stoic, and in control. That emotions were weakness. That tenderness was reserved for women. But Katrina shattered that illusion. She taught me that real strength is gentle. That protection isn't about dominance—it's about presence. That masculinity can be soft, nurturing, and deeply emotional.

I didn't have to be hard to be a good father. I had to be honest. I had to be present. I had to be willing to love without fear.

Katrina gave me that gift.

She taught me that fatherhood isn't just about provision—it's about connection. It's about showing up, listening, and letting your children see your heart. She helped me break free from the rigid mold I had inherited and step into a version of manhood that was whole, compassionate, and true.

And every time I saw her smile, every time she reached for me, every time she rested her head on my shoulder—I knew I was becoming the man I was meant to be.

Maria Lakeisha Oglesby – A New Beginning

By December 1997, I had been working in the City of Decatur's Street Department for six years. When I first joined, I met Jay Glenn—a country boy from Cordele, Georgia, with arms like a bodybuilder and a work ethic that could humble anyone. Jay wasn't book-smart, but he was brilliant with his hands. He could operate heavy machinery, lay bricks, finish concrete, build forms—you name it, Jay could do it.

When I transferred from Grounds Maintenance, Jay took me under his wing. I didn't mind hard work, and I learned quickly. Within five years, I could do everything Jay could do. I was proud of that.

I was earning about $400 a week doing city work, but I started to think—what if I could make $400 per job working for private citizens? So, I made flyers advertising concrete, brick, stone, and stucco work. At the top, I wrote Concrete Specialist.

I was proud of that flyer. It represented my leap of faith, my desire to build something of my own. I showed it to the "Man of God," hoping for encouragement.

Instead, he mocked me.

He held up my flyer in front of the entire congregation and said, "This is another example of how high-minded Michael is. He's calling himself a 'Specialist' when he's not a specialist." The congregation laughed.

For years, they called me "Specialist" as a joke—a nickname meant to humiliate me.

I couldn't understand why he ridiculed me. He had encouraged others to start landscaping businesses. But the difference was, this idea didn't come from him. If he wasn't the originator, he couldn't support it.

But I didn't let that stop me.

I took my flyers to Buckhead, one of Atlanta's most affluent neighborhoods, and passed them out. The calls started coming in. At first, I worked evenings after my city job, but soon I had so many clients that I gave my two weeks' notice and stepped into full-time self-employment.

My wife was eight and a half months pregnant with our fourth child.

On January 8, 1998—my last day at the City of Decatur—I got a call around midday. Her water had broken. I rushed to the hospital, and that day, **Maria Lakeisha Oglesby** was born.

We named her after the "Man of God's" second wife, Mary—Maria in Spanish.

I call her my January 8th baby. Her birthday marks the day I left behind a job and stepped into a new life. It's a date I'll never forget.

Maria was stunning, with thick, dark brown hair, a voice like an angel. She could sing, play piano, and light up a room. My wife and I adored her.

But the "Man of God" didn't.

He mocked her. Called her ugly. Said she wasn't smart. And I—ashamedly—did nothing. I didn't defend her. I let it happen. I was a coward.

But my cowardice wouldn't last forever.

I let him speak those words over my daughter. I was afraid. I was silent. But Maria wasn't.

She grew up with grace, intelligence, and determination. She didn't let the words spoken over her define her. She rose above them.

Maria went on to graduate Magna Cum Laude from Valdosta State University. She didn't just succeed; she excelled. And today, she teaches English classes in Europe, sharing her voice, her brilliance, and her story with the world.

She became everything they said she couldn't be.

And I've never been prouder.

Maria taught me that silence can be broken. That dignity can be reclaimed. That even when you don't speak up in the moment, you can still honor someone by telling their truth later.

She is my daughter. My teacher. My reminder that love wins.

Nickolas Mekail Oglesby – My Birthday Blessing

By the time our fifth child was on the way, people had started asking me the same question over and over:

"Why do you and your wife have so many kids?"

"Aren't you worried about how expensive children are?"

My answer was always the same: "If God gave us twenty children, He would make a way for us to provide for them."

I believed that with every fiber of my being. My children were gifts from God, and I was determined to care for each one. The scriptures say that Jesus fed five thousand with two fish and five loaves of bread—so providing for my little family was nothing for Him.

I said it with conviction, and even the "Man of God" would get excited when I spoke those words before the congregation.

I believed in a rich God, the kind who owns the cattle on a thousand hills. And I believed that if you find your passion and work hard to perfect it, God will give you access to those riches.

On May 12, 1999—just one day after my birthday—my wife gave birth to our fifth child, a son: **Nickolas Mekail Oglesby.** It was the most beautiful birthday gift I could have received from God and my wife.

Nickolas was bald but handsome, with a calm spirit. He didn't cry much and was easy to care for. As he grew, he became the kind of child who could entertain himself for hours. All he needed were his toys and his imagination. I saw myself in him—just like I had been with my He-Man, Stretch Armstrong, ThunderCats, and toy cars.

Our relationship has always felt like more than just father and son—we're buddies. We watch movies together and love to talk about them afterward. One of our favorites was Small Soldiers, a film about toy soldiers brought to life by computer chips.

In one scene, a character named Nick Nitro was destroyed during a mission. The commander shouted, "Bring me the head of Nick Nitro!"

We laughed so hard at that moment that I started calling Nickolas "Nick Nitro." And even now, as a grown man, I still call him that sometimes. It's our thing—a nickname born from a shared memory, a bond that's never faded.

Nickolas is a reminder that fatherhood isn't just about provision—it's about connection. It's about finding joy in the small things, building trust through time, and creating memories that last a lifetime.

Cameron Oglesby – Grace in Motion

After Nickolas was born, life kept moving—full of work, family, and the steady rhythm of raising children. People still asked, "How many kids are you going to have?" And I still answered with conviction, "If God gave us twenty, He'd make a way."

I believed it. I lived it. And once again, God blessed us.

My wife became pregnant with our sixth child, and by then, I had learned to embrace each new arrival with gratitude and anticipation. I didn't worry about provision; I trusted in it. I didn't fear the future; I prepared for it. My children were not just part of my life; they were my purpose.

On the day **Cameron Oglesby** was born, I felt that familiar wave of awe—the moment when you hold your child for the first time and realize that love has expanded again. Cameron was beautiful, his own person from the start, yet another reflection of the grace that had carried us this far.

He was calm, observant, and full of quiet strength. I remember looking into his eyes and feeling the weight of responsibility settle deeper into my spirit. Another soul to guide. Another heart to protect. Another legacy to nurture.

With Cameron, I felt a renewed sense of purpose. He

arrived at a time when I was growin; not just as a father, but as a man. My business was thriving, my faith was strong, and my understanding of fatherhood had matured. I knew now that being a father wasn't just about providing—it was about presence. About listening. About showing up with love every single day.

Cameron fit right into the rhythm of our family. He was surrounded by siblings, laughter, and the kind of love that multiplies, not divides. And as he grew, I saw pieces of myself in him—my quiet moments, my curiosity, my drive.

He reminded me that every child is a new beginning. A new chance to love better, lead wiser, and live more fully.

Cameron – The Road Back

Cameron came into this world with quiet strength and a gentle spirit. From the beginning, he was different. He required more patience, more understanding, more grace. And I gave it—because I saw something in him. Something good. Something worth waiting for.

As he grew older, Cameron faced challenges that tested him—and tested me. He got himself into serious trouble. He veered off the path we had tried to lay before him. There were moments when I didn't know what to do. Moments when I felt helpless, angry, and afraid. But never hopeless.

Because even in the darkest seasons, I could still see the goodness in his heart.

I saw it in the way he loved his siblings. In the way he could make us laugh. In the quiet moments when he let his guard down and showed me glimpses of the boy I knew was still in there.

Cameron reminded me that fatherhood isn't just about celebrating the easy victories—it's about standing firm in the storms. It's about loving your child when they're hardest to love. It's about believing in them when they've stopped believing in themselves.

I've had to learn patience in a deeper way with Cameron. Not the kind that waits for a toddler to stop crying, but the kind that waits for a soul to find its way back. The kind that doesn't give up, even when the world says you should.

And I still believe in him.

I believe that when it's all said and done, Cameron will find his way to the high road. I believe that the lessons he's learning now will shape him into a man of strength, wisdom, and compassion. I believe that his story isn't finished—and that the best chapters are still ahead.

Because love doesn't quit. And neither do I.

Linda Patricia Oglesby – A Name, A Spirit, A Stand

Five months after Cameron was born, my wife was pregnant again. True to our pattern—two boys, two girls, two boys—the seventh child was a girl. By that time, I had made peace with the rhythm of our growing family. I didn't worry about gender anymore. I just prayed for health, safety, and a smooth delivery.

In February of 2002, **Linda Patricia Oglesby** was born.

We named her after my mother, though I can't say exactly why we chose that name. But looking back, it feels divinely inspired. Linda looks like my mother, sings like my mother, and talks like my mother. She's the most like her of all my daughters. Maybe names carry more than meaning—maybe they carry spirit.

When it was time to bring my wife and baby Linda home from the hospital, I wanted to do something special. She had just given birth to our seventh child. She had endured pain, sacrifice and brought another life into the world. So I took her to a nice restaurant on the way home. Next door was a movie theater, and we decided to watch a film together, just the two of us and our newborn daughter.

It was a beautiful moment. A celebration of life, love, and gratitude.

But joy doesn't always go unpunished.

Someone told the "Man of God" what we had done. That night at Bible study, he confronted me in front of the entire congregation. "Michael, how is it that the first place you took your wife after delivery was a restaurant?" He declared that the first place a woman should go after childbirth was the church, or else stay home until she was ready to attend.

I stood my ground. I told him, "I don't see anything wrong with feeding my wife and showing her gratitude for the suffering she endured to bring our daughter into this world."

He threatened to disfellowship me if I didn't agree with his new rule.

But I knew what was right. I knew what love looked like. And I knew that God had been with us in that delivery room, just as He had been for every birth. I had knelt beside my wife, prayed with all my heart, and watched God bring her through safely every time.

All my children were born healthy, mentally and physically. And I wasn't going to let anyone shame me for celebrating that.

Linda's birth wasn't just another addition to our family. It was a moment of clarity. A moment where love stood taller than control. A moment where I began to see that honoring your wife, your children, and your God doesn't always look the way others expect it to.

Sometimes, it looks like dinner and a movie. Sometimes, it looks like quiet resistance. And sometimes, it looks like a baby girl named Linda, carrying the spirit of her grandmother, the strength of her mother, and the love of a father who refused to be silenced.

Courtney Leanne Oglesby – Grace in the Midst of Strain

In the summer of 2003, about a year after Linda was born, my wife became pregnant with our eighth child. True to our pattern—two boys, two girls, two boys, two girls—it was another daughter. By that time, I had come to embrace the rhythm of our growing family. Gender didn't matter anymore. What mattered was health—hers and the baby's.

But something had changed.

I began to notice the toll that childbearing was taking on my wife. Her teeth were losing density, likely from the calcium drained during pregnancy. She walked with a slight limp, the result of pelvic strain from carrying so many children. And while she remained a beautiful woman—so much so that people were shocked to learn she was the mother of seven, soon to be eight—I saw the hidden costs. The ones most people couldn't see.

Pregnancy takes from a woman in ways that aren't always visible. And as her husband, I felt helpless. I wanted to give her more time between pregnancies. I wanted to protect her health. But because of the teachings of the "Man of God," I was powerless.

Though I've always been pro-life, I also believe in wisdom. I would have considered some form of planned parenthood, not to reject life, but to preserve the life of the woman who was giving so much of herself. But even suggesting birth control would have led to swift condemnation. My wife would have reported me to the "Man of God" and the congregation without hesitation.

And so, I stayed silent. Troubled. Watching her suffer.

In February of 2004, she gave birth to our eighth child: **Courtney Leanne Oglesby.**

Courtney's delivery was smooth, and she entered the world with beautiful eyes and dimples that could lift your spirit. She was quiet, observant, and deeply intelligent—surprising us with how quickly she learned and how naturally she carried herself.

Her mother named her simply because she loved the name. And it fit. Courtney has always had a quiet ambition, an entrepreneurial spirit, and a spark that hints at future success. I believe she's destined to be a businesswoman—driven, focused, and full of grace.

Her birth marked another chapter in our journey. A moment of joy in the midst of concern. A reminder that even when life feels heavy, love continues to grow.

Courtney Leanne Oglesby – From Dimples to Duty

Courtney Leanne Oglesby entered our lives with quiet grace and radiant dimples. From the beginning, she carried herself with calm confidence. She was observant, intelligent, and had a smile that could lift your spirit on the darkest day.

As she grew, her ambition became clear. She had the heart of a leader and the mind of a visionary. We always believed she'd become a successful businesswoman, but Courtney had another calling.

She joined the United States Navy, stepping into a life of service, discipline, and global responsibility. She served aboard the **USS Dwight D. Eisenhower (CVN-69)**, one of the Navy's most powerful aircraft carriers. The Eisenhower is a floating city, a symbol of American strength, and Courtney was part of its heartbeat.

Watching her step into uniform was one of the proudest moments of my life. She wasn't just my daughter anymore; she was a sailor, a protector, a woman of valor.

Her journey reminds me that strength comes in many forms. Sometimes it's quiet. Sometimes it's bold. Sometimes it's wrapped in a Navy uniform, standing tall on the deck of a warship.

Courtney's story is still unfolding, but one thing is certain: she carries the legacy of our family with honor. And wherever she sails, she takes a piece of our love with her.

Patience Nicole Oglesby – The Strong One

In the winter of 2004, my wife was expecting our ninth child. By then, I had come to rely on a familiar pattern: two boys, two girls, two boys, two girls. Naturally, I assumed this child would be a boy. That's how it had gone so far, right?

Wrong.

We found out we were expecting another girl—and just like that, the pattern was broken. But by this point, I didn't mind. I had learned that gender didn't matter as long as my wife and the baby were healthy. What did matter was that I felt like I was going to be buying diapers for the rest of my life. As soon as one child was potty-trained, another was born to take their place. It was a never-ending cycle of wipes, bottles, and late-night feedings.

In **July of 2005**, **Patience Nicole Oglesby** was born.

From the beginning, Patience showed signs of being one of my strongest children. She was sweet, yes, but strong-willed, determined, and full of personality. I'll never forget one day when my wife and I were sitting on the porch with her. Patience started pretending she was the parent, and we were her kids. She made imaginary food and began feeding us.

"Are you hungry?" she asked.

"No," I replied.

"Yes, you are! Eat!" she insisted.

Then she turned to my wife: "Are you hungry?" Before my wife could answer, Patience commanded, "Yes, you are! Eat!"

We laughed so hard. It was adorable, and it was Patience. She wasn't going to be a pushover. She knew what she wanted, and she made sure you knew it, too.

She wasn't just strong-willed; she was physically strong. Not long ago, we went to a swimming pool, and Patience challenged me to a race. Now, I grew up at the Boys' Club. I was trained to swim and considered myself a strong swimmer. Patience had never been trained.

I accepted the challenge, confident I'd win.

She beat me. Easily.

That's Patience. She defies expectations. She surprises you. She pushes boundaries. And she does it all with a smile that could melt the hardest heart.

She may have broken the pattern, but she built something even better—a legacy of strength, spirit, and joy.

When Boldness Became Contagious

From the moment **Patience Nicole Oglesby** arrived, she carried herself with a kind of authority that was rare in someone so young. She wasn't loud or unruly; she was decisive. Strong-willed. Unapologetically herself. And that energy didn't just stay with her—it rippled through the house.

In a family of nine children, it's easy for personalities to blur, for younger siblings to follow the lead of older ones. But Patience broke that mold. She didn't wait for permission to lead; she just did. Whether she was pretending to be the parent on the porch or challenging me to a swimming race she had no formal training for (and winning), Patience made it clear: she was here to be heard.

Her boldness gave her siblings permission to be more expressive. It shifted the tone of family conversations. Suddenly, the younger ones weren't afraid to speak up. They saw Patience stand her ground, and they realized they could too. She didn't just influence her siblings; she empowered them.

Even her older brothers and sisters took notice. They learned that strength didn't always come from age or experience; sometimes it comes from conviction. Patience reminded all of us that leadership isn't assigned; it's earned, moment by moment, through courage and clarity.

And for me, as a father, her boldness was a mirror. It challenged me to listen more deeply, to respond more thoughtfully, and to recognize that sometimes the smallest voices carry the biggest truths.

Patience didn't just add to the family, she recalibrated it. She brought balance to the dynamic, reminding everyone that strength can be sweet, and that boldness, when rooted in love, can be the glue that holds a family together.

Shiphrah Cierre Oglesby – The Spirit of a Midwife

In the first chapter of Exodus, the Bible tells the story of two Hebrew midwives—Shiphrah and Puah. These women were entrusted with overseeing the births of Hebrew children during a time of brutal oppression under Pharaoh, the king of Egypt. Fearing the rapid growth and strength of the Israelites, Pharaoh ordered the midwives to kill every male child born to the Hebrews.

But Shiphrah and Puah feared God more than they feared Pharaoh. They refused to carry out his wicked command. They saved the boy children alive, and because of their courage, God blessed them, and the children of Israel grew mighty.

On December 1, 2006, my wife gave birth to our tenth child—a beautiful baby girl. We named her **Shiphrah**, in honor of the midwife who defied tyranny and protected life.

What's remarkable is how fitting that name turned out to be.

From an early age, Shiphrah showed a deep passion for caring for babies. She currently works in a nursery and dreams of one day owning her own. It's as if the spirit of the biblical Shiphrah lives in her: gentle, nurturing, and fiercely protective.

But Shiphrah isn't just compassionate, she's magnetic. She reminds me of my wife's two older brothers, who had a way of lighting up a room with laughter and playfulness. Whenever they came around, they lifted my spirits. Shiphrah has that same gift. She's a natural comedian, full of charm and joy. When she walks into a room, the atmosphere changes. She makes people smile. She makes people feel good.

She was our tenth child. After her birth, I met a man who asked me how many children I had. I told him, "Ten." He smiled and said, "You don't have just a family; you have a tribe."

I liked that. I carried it with pride.

Because Shiphrah wasn't just another child, she was

a symbol of legacy, laughter, and life. She carried a name rooted in resistance and righteousness, and she lived it out with grace and joy.

Tribe of Ten – Redefining Fatherhood

When Shiphrah was born—our tenth child—I crossed a threshold I hadn't fully anticipated. I wasn't just a father anymore. I was the father of a tribe.

I remember a man asking me how many children I had. I told him, "Ten." He smiled and said, "You don't have just a family—you have a tribe." Something about that stuck with me. It felt right. It felt true.

Reaching ten children didn't just change my perspective on fatherhood; it redefined it.

In the beginning, fatherhood felt like a role. I was the provider, the protector, the teacher. I had responsibilities, and I took them seriously. But with each child, something deeper began to take root. By the time I held my tenth baby in my arms, I realized I wasn't just guiding a few lives, I was stewarding a legacy.

I learned that love doesn't divide; it multiplies. Patience isn't something you're born with; it's something you build day by day, through sleepless nights, scraped knees, and whispered prayers. I discovered that being a father isn't about control, it's about consistency. It's about showing up—even when you're tired, even when you're unsure, even when you feel like you're failing.

Ten children taught me that every child is a universe. Each comes with their own rhythm, their own voice, their own way of seeing the world. Some are quiet thinkers, some are bold leaders. Some need a gentle nudge, others need space to soar. I had to learn to adapt, to listen, to lead with humility.

I also saw the toll it took on my wife, and that deepened my empathy. I began to understand that fatherhood wasn't just about my relationship with my children; it was about honoring the woman who brought them into the world. I became more protective of her, more grateful for her, more aware of the sacrifices she made in silence.

And perhaps most importantly, ten children taught me that fatherhood is spiritual. It's not just about diapers and discipline. It's about legacy, faith, and the quiet hope that your children will carry forward the best parts of you—and leave behind the rest.

I didn't just become a father of ten. I became a father with depth, with vision, and with a heart big enough to hold a tribe.

A Father Among Many – How My Tribe Shaped My Identity

By the time Shiphrah was born—our tenth child—something began to shift. Not just in our household, but in how I was seen by others. I wasn't just Michael anymore. I was Michael, the man with ten kids. The father of a tribe.

In the community, people started to take notice. Strangers would ask how many children I had, and when I said ten, their eyes would widen. Some were amazed. Some were skeptical. Some were inspired. But no one was indifferent. My family had become a statement—of faith, of commitment, of endurance.

In the church, my identity evolved even more. I was no longer just a member of the congregation, I was seen as a symbol of spiritual fruitfulness. The "Man of God" would sometimes praise me publicly for being fruitful and multiplying, quoting scriptures that affirmed large families as a blessing. Other times, he used my family as a cautionary tale, especially when he felt I was stepping out of line. Either way, I had become visible.

People began to associate me with fatherhood itself. Young men would approach me for advice. Older members would comment on how well-behaved my children were. Some would ask how I managed it all—how I provided, how I stayed sane, how I kept the faith.

And truthfully, I didn't always have the answers. But I had experience. I had love. I had stories.

My tribe gave me credibility. It gave me a platform. It gave me a voice.

But it also gave me responsibility. I knew that every action I took reflected not just on me, but on my wife, my children, and the values we lived by. I had to be mindful of how I spoke, how I led, how I responded to conflict. I had to be more patient, more thoughtful, more intentional.

Fatherhood had become my ministry.

And as my tribe grew, so did my understanding of leadership. I wasn't just leading a family—I was shaping a legacy. I was building something that would outlive me. And that realization changed everything.

Fatherhood and the Breaking of Chains

As my family grew, so did my understanding of what it meant to be a father. With each child, I wasn't just learning how to change diapers or manage bedtime routines, I was learning how to lead, how to protect, and how to discern. And slowly, that leadership began to extend beyond my household.

Fatherhood taught me to listen to my own voice.

For years, I had submitted to the authority of the "Man of God." His teachings shaped my decisions, his approval guided my actions, and his disapproval could shake my confidence. But as I became a father to more children, something began to shift. I started to see that the same discernment I used to guide my children was the same discernment I needed to apply to my spiritual life.

I began to question—not out of rebellion, but out of responsibility.

I had children watching me. I had a wife depending on me. I couldn't afford to blindly follow teachings that didn't align with the Word of God or with the well-being of my family. I started reading Scripture for myself, not just to confirm what I'd been told, but to understand what God was truly telling me.

And what I found was clarity.

I realized that leadership in the home required humility, wisdom, and love. But leadership in the church often demanded submission, silence, and fear. That contradiction began to trouble me. I couldn't reconcile the nurturing, protective role I played at home with the passive, unquestioning role I was expected to play in the congregation.

Fatherhood made me bold.

I started to speak up more, to challenge teachings that didn't sit right, to protect my family not just physically, but spiritually. And with every act of courage, I felt a little freer—a little more connected to God, a little more confident in the path He was laying before me.

My relationship with church authority became

strained. The "Man of God" didn't like being questioned. He saw my independence as arrogance and labeled me "high-minded." But I knew better. I wasn't trying to exalt myself; I was trying to honor the truth. I wanted to be the kind of father my children could trust, the kind of man my wife could lean on, the kind of believer God could use.

Fatherhood didn't just change how I led my family—it changed how I followed God.

And in that shift, I found something priceless: spiritual independence. Not isolation. Not rebellion. But a quiet, steady walk with God—one that wasn't filtered through fear or control. A walk rooted in love, truth, and the sacred responsibility of being a father.

Kiera Lynn Oglesby – My Sweet Muffin

In December of 2007, my wife became pregnant with our eleventh child. By then, we had weathered many pregnancies together, but something about this one felt different. I could see it in the way she walked, with a distinct limp caused by strain on her pelvic bone. I could see it in her feet, swollen so badly it made me cringe. And I could feel it in my gut, this pregnancy was going to be harder than the rest.

She developed gestational diabetes, and her body was clearly under stress. Up until this point, she had carried each child with grace and strength, but this time, I saw her struggle. And as her husband, it troubled me deeply.

In August of 2008, she went into labor. I rushed her to the hospital, and what followed were hours of agonizing pain. I sat beside her, helpless, feeling every contraction in my spirit. For the first time in all her deliveries, she cried. She had never shed a tear during labor before, but this time, the pain broke through.

My mother was in the delivery room, as she always was. The doctor overseeing the birth was a young white woman with a gentle spirit and a kind bedside manner. She informed us that the baby was breech—coming feet first instead of headfirst—and that a C-section might be necessary.

Until then, all of our children had been born naturally. But in our church, the "Man of God" taught that a C-section was a punishment from God. Women who had them were frowned upon by the congregation. That belief weighed heavily on us. We didn't want judgment; we wanted grace.

So I did what I knew to do. I got down on my knees in the delivery room and prayed. I asked God to help my wife deliver naturally. I asked Him to turn the baby.

The young doctor heard me praying. She placed one hand on my wife's belly and reached into her womb with the other. And with care and skill, she turned the baby around.

My wife delivered naturally.

When Kiera Lynn Oglesby arrived, I was overwhelmed with relief and joy. She had a head full of black hair and the sweetest disposition. Even as a baby, she smiled often. You could tell she was going to be full of personality.

I remember watching her sleep. She'd stir, open her eyes, see me, and immediately flash the biggest, warmest smile. It melted me every time. That smile was her gift to me, and because of it, I gave her a name of my own: **Muffin.**

She was soft, sweet, and full of joy. And after all the pain and fear, she reminded me that love always rises—like a muffin in the oven, warm and comforting.

Philip Miguel Oglesby – The Sacred Twelve

In February of 2009, my wife was pregnant with our twelfth child. By then, the questions and criticisms had become routine. "Why so many kids?" "How do you afford it?" "Aren't you overwhelmed?"

But I had an answer, one rooted in scripture and conviction. Jesus chose twelve disciples. Jacob had twelve sons, who became the twelve tribes of Israel. In the New Heaven, there are twelve gates, each guarded by an angel, and each gate made of a single pearl. The number twelve carries divine weight. It represents order, completeness, and spiritual authority.

So when people questioned me, I didn't flinch. I saw my twelve children not as excess, but as purpose.

In November of 2009, my wife went into labor for the twelfth time. I took her to the hospital, where she was assigned a young white male doctor. He was kind, calm, and immediately put me at ease. He guided my wife through each breath, each push, with gentle precision.

As he worked, I did what I always did: I got down on my knees and prayed. I asked God to bless my wife, to strengthen her, to bring our child safely into the world.

And then something extraordinary happened.

The doctor began to pray with me.

"Father, in the name of Jesus, bless this young woman and give her the strength to birth her baby into this world."

I was stunned. In that sterile hospital room, surrounded by machines and monitors, heaven touched earth. A doctor—trained in science—joined me in faith. It was a moment I'll never forget.

Not long after, **Philip Miguel Oglesby** was born. He had a full head of black hair and looked almost identical to his brother Cameron as a baby. He was handsome, healthy, and perfect.

And with his arrival, I now had a wife and twelve children—a full tribe. I felt the weight of that responsibility, but I never shied away from it. I had complete faith that God would make a way for us to live a good life. I believed I was anointed to be a father and husband, and I embraced that calling with everything I had.

To me, my children were special. Each one carried a unique gift, a divine spark meant to bless the world. I was determined to create an environment where they could grow, thrive, and fulfill their purpose.

But I also began to realize something deeper: to give my children a fair chance at life, I would have to pay a price—not just financially, but spiritually, emotionally, and sometimes socially. I would have to stand against criticism, endure judgment, and sacrifice comfort. I would have to fight for their futures, even when the world didn't understand.

And I was willing. Because fatherhood wasn't just my role; it was my ministry. And Philip, the twelfth, was the seal of that calling.

The Price of Protection – Sacrifices for My Children's Futures

By the time **Philip Miguel Oglesby** was born—my twelfth child—I had crossed into a new realm of fatherhood. I wasn't just raising children anymore. I was stewarding destinies. And with that realization came a sobering truth: protecting their futures would require sacrifice.

Not just the kind people expect—money, time, sleep. Those were givens. I'm talking about the deeper sacrifices—the ones that cost your comfort, your reputation, your peace of mind.

I began to sacrifice my **silence.**

There were moments in church when I knew the teachings didn't align with the Word of God or the well-being of my family. I had once held my tongue out of fear, out of respect, out of habit. But now, with twelve children watching me, I couldn't afford to stay silent. I had to speak up. I had to model courage, even when it meant being labeled "high-minded," even when it meant standing alone.

I sacrificed my **image.**

People judged me for having so many children. They assumed irresponsibility, chaos, and poverty. They didn't see the structure, the love, the intentionality. I had to let go of the need to be understood. I had to accept that my life wouldn't fit into their boxes. I learned to wear their judgment like armor and keep walking.

I sacrificed my **ease.**

There were easier paths—smaller families, simpler routines, fewer mouths to feed. But I didn't choose ease, I chose purpose. I chose to believe that each child was a gift, and that my calling was to nurture those gifts into greatness. That meant long hours, hard work, and constant prayer. It meant being tired but still present. Giving, even when I had little left.

I sacrificed my **independence.**

There were dreams I put on hold, opportunities I passed up, and moments I gave away so my children could have theirs. I didn't resent it—I embraced it. Because fatherhood isn't about what you keep; it's about what you give.

And I gave everything.

Because I believe in my children. I believe that each one carries something sacred. I believe that God entrusted them to me not just to raise, but to protect, to guide, and to prepare.

And if that meant sacrificing my comfort, my pride, or my place in the crowd—so be it.

Because the price of protection is high. But the reward is eternal.

CHAPTER 10
THE GRAVEYARD

I once heard a speech—a sad one. I can't remember for the life of me who gave it, but it was about how many young people die before they even reach adulthood, ending up in graveyards long before their time. But what struck me most wasn't just that they died young. The speaker asked a question that has stayed with me ever since:

How many dreams, gifts, and untapped potentials were buried with them?

That was the heartbreaking part of the speech.

I've come to liken the Man of God's organization to a kind of graveyard. When I think about it, the same question rises in my mind: how many dreams have died there? How many gifts were never realized? How many goals and destinies were buried before they even had a chance to live?

When I think of the hundreds of children born into that organization, I can't help but wonder—why aren't there any teachers among them? Why aren't there any doctors, lawyers, or judges? Why are there no professionals shaping the world beyond the walls of that church?

Thoughts like these began to stir in me after I became the father of twelve children. I had seven girls, and within the Man of God's congregation, the highest aspiration for a girl was to become a wife and mother as soon as possible—often at the age of fourteen.

Now, I believe that being a wife and mother is an honorable calling, one deserving of respect. But it's not the only calling a woman can have. There are women who are doctors, lawyers, judges, counselors, therapists, nurses, teachers—even a woman has served as Vice President of the United States. I wanted those possibilities to be available to my daughters, too.

But the Man of God's teachings forbade such ambitions. His doctrine closed every door that led beyond his control. Yet I knew my children had potential—God-given intelligence and creativity that deserved to be nurtured, not buried. I wanted all of them to be educated because I knew they could excel. That ability was something passed down from my father, through me, to them.

Just as Martin Luther King Jr. once said, I, too, had a dream.

But I found myself in a position of weakness. Even though I was the father, provider, and caretaker of my family, the Man of God held all the power in my home. It was power he had slowly gained over the years I spent under his teachings—teachings that began shaping me when I was just four years old.

My stepfather and mother had drilled into me the importance of total submission to him, and I carried that same mindset into my own household. I taught my children to do the same. My wife and I instructed them to show loyalty first to the Man of God. Even if conflict arose between us as their parents and him as their spiritual leader, we told them their loyalty should still lie with him.

Looking back, I see that every ounce of power he held over my wife and children was power I had given him.

And that realization was devastating.

I had the responsibility to provide for my family, but not the authority to lead them. Brother Allen had that authority. He shaped their thinking, their choices, their futures.

So I began to ask myself the question that haunts me to this day:

Was this world the Man of God created nothing more than a graveyard of dreams—especially for my children?

Catch Him in the Act – When Doctrine Becomes Deception

To understand the Man of God, you must first understand his origin. His entire theology was built on one central doctrine: whoever is filled with the Holy Ghost cannot commit sin.

This belief wasn't born in isolation—it was passed down from his uncle, who was both his spiritual mentor and a preacher himself. His uncle taught that once a person was filled with the Holy Spirit, they became incapable of sin.

On the surface, it sounds righteous. Innocent, even.

But in practice, it was dangerous.

Why?

Because when a person believes they are incapable of sin, they stop being honest with themselves and with others. And when they inevitably fall short of that impossible standard, they don't repent. They rationalize. They create "mysteries" and "revelations" to cover their wrongdoing. They twist scripture to protect their image.

Let me give you an example.

The Man of God's uncle preached that he was Holy

Ghost-filled and therefore sinless. Yet behind closed doors, he was having sexual relationships with multiple women in his congregation—women who were married to other men.

One of those men was a mechanic. A "shade tree" mechanic who worked on cars right in his front yard. The uncle would visit under the pretense of prayer and ministry. While the husband worked outside, he would be inside the house with the man's wife—sometimes pressed against a wall near the window, keeping an eye out to make sure he wasn't caught.

Other times, he'd sit in a living room chair and have the woman straddle him. And if the husband happened to walk in, he'd place his hand on her forehead and pretend to be praying.

He used prayer as a cover for adultery.

So how did he justify it?

He claimed God had given him a revelation. He said that because both he and the women were filled with the Holy Ghost, they were "clean." And if two clean sheets rub together, he reasoned, they can't make each other dirty.

"So how can two Holy Ghost-filled people sin against each other?" he asked.

That was his so-called mystery—his divine loophole, his spiritual cover for sin.

But it wasn't divine. It was deception.

This is what happens when unrealistic expectations

are placed on human beings, especially in the name of God. It leads to dishonesty, to manipulation, to spiritual abuse. And when people are taught that they cannot sin, they stop seeking truth. They start hiding behind it.

This chapter isn't just about one man's corruption. It's about the danger of elevating doctrine above accountability. It's about the cost of blind faith.

And it's about the courage it takes to call it out.

Catch Him in the Act – The Fall of a False Prophet

In my line of work as a heating and air technician, I've learned that some problems are tricky. A system might seem fine when I arrive, but the issue only shows itself when the conditions are just right. So I tell my customers, "Call me when it's malfunctioning—so I can catch it in the act."

That principle doesn't just apply to machines. It applies to people. Especially the tricky ones.

The "Man of God's" uncle was one of those people. He preached that anyone filled with the Holy Ghost could not commit sin. It was a doctrine passed down from his own pastor—his uncle—and it became the foundation of his ministry. But behind the pulpit, his uncle and pastor was committing adultery with multiple women in his congregation, married women.

He was clever. If accused, he'd lie. If confronted, he'd twist scripture. He used prayer as a disguise, placing his hand on a woman's forehead mid-act if her husband walked in, pretending to be ministering.

But eventually, the husbands had had enough.

They devised a plan. One of the women agreed to lure the uncle into a sexual rendezvous. She called him, and he came quickly. Once inside, they began to engage in sex. That's when the husbands burst into the room, cameras flashing. They took photos, seized his clothes, and refused to return them until they had all the evidence they needed.

Then they posted the photos all over town.

The "Man of God" didn't participate in the setup—he loved his uncle too much. But the damage was done. The uncle lost his congregation. The church shut down.

One husband wasn't satisfied. He wanted personal justice. He went to confront the uncle face-to-face.

"I just have to hit you one time to feel better," he said.

He swung—a right hook—but only grazed the uncle's chin. He swung again.

But the uncle was tricky.

He had hung a housecoat over the bedroom door, with a knife hidden in the pocket. When the second punch came, he reached into the coat, pulled the knife, and stabbed the man in the gut.

The man ran down the street, clutching his stomach, seeking help. He survived—and pressed charges.

The uncle was arrested and faced attempted murder charges. With the help of his loyal nephew, Brother Allen, he hired a lawyer and went to trial.

During the proceedings, it was revealed that he had been sleeping with some of these women for up to five years. One woman testified, "I was hypnotized by him. He used the name of God to hypnotize me."

The lawyer responded sarcastically, "That's the longest hypnosis I've ever heard of."

The courtroom erupted in laughter—even the judge chuckled.

But anyone who's dealt with a cult leader knows there's truth in that statement.

People often accused the "Man of God" of running a cult. His response was always the same: "If I'm running a cult, where are the chains? Where are the fences? Where are the armed guards?"

But the chains were there. Not around wrists—around minds.

Invisible. Psychological. Spiritual.

The uncle was found not guilty by reason of self-defense. But the damage was done. The illusion was shattered.

And for many, the healing had only just begun.

Throw a Mystery on Them – Smoke and Mirrors in the Pulpit

Eventually, the "Man of God" broke away from his uncle and started a congregation of his own. But make no mistake—he didn't leave the teachings behind. He was his uncle's star pupil, and he carried forward the same manipulative tactics that had defined his mentor's ministry.

One of the most effective techniques he inherited was something his uncle called throwing a mystery on them.

It was a psychological maneuver, a spiritual smokescreen—a way to escape accountability when cornered in conflict.

His uncle taught, "If you're losing an argument, don't defend yourself—throw a mystery on them."

The goal was simple: confuse the opposition. Shift the focus. Instead of addressing the real issue, the opponent would get tangled in debating the mystery. The argument would dissolve into theological riddles, abstract revelations, and spiritual detours. And just like that, the truth would be buried.

The "Man of God" mastered this technique.

He used it most effectively during a heated battle with Fulton County DFCS. The details of the case were serious—questions of cruelty to children, child welfare, family integrity, and institutional oversight. But instead of confronting the issue directly, he threw a mystery.

He cloaked the conflict in divine language. He preached that the attack wasn't from DFCS—it was from Satan. That the investigation wasn't about abusing children; it was about a parent's right to discipline or spank their children. That the accusations weren't legal, they were prophetic. He threw a mystery on Fulton County DFCS and the world!

And just like that, the congregation rallied behind him. They weren't defending a man—they were defending a mystery. A parent's right to discipline their children.

The original issue was lost in the fog.

This is the danger of unchecked spiritual authority: when doctrine becomes a tool of deflection, when mystery replaces accountability, when charisma overrides character, truth becomes the casualty.

And the people? They're left debating shadows. While the real conflict goes unresolved.

Swinging for the Fences – When Violence Wears a Collar

There's a scene in Pulp Fiction that's hard to forget. Two characters—Ving Rhames and Bruce Willis—are bound and gagged in a basement. One of the captors says,

"Bring out the Gimp." The Gimp is a masked, violent figure kept in a cage, used for one purpose only.

The "Man of God" had his own version of the Gimp.

He wasn't kept in a cage. He didn't wear a mask. But he was used for one purpose only—to deliver brutal beatings.

One night during Bible study, a mother brought up a concern. Her son's teacher had called several times, reporting that the boy was unruly and disruptive in class. The "Man of God" didn't tolerate children undermining authority. So he called the boy—only seven years old—to the front of the church.

When asked why he misbehaved, the boy had no answer. He was confused, overwhelmed, and standing before a room full of adults. But instead of compassion, he was met with violence.

The "Man of God" ordered four men to grab the child—one on each limb—and hold him spread-eagled in the air. Then he summoned the enforcer, a large, physically imposing man known for one thing: swinging belts with terrifying force.

And swing he did.

You ever hear someone say a baseball player is "swinging for the fences"? It means he's not aiming for a base hit—or even a triple—he's trying to knock the ball out of the park. That's how this man swung the belt. Not with restraint. Not as a correction. But with the full force of rage and control.

The boy's body was left covered in bruises, lacerations, and open wounds. And it didn't stop until the "Man of God" gave the order.

This wasn't discipline. It was domination. It was a reenactment of slave-master brutality, carried out in a place that claimed to be holy. It revealed the darkest side of unchecked spiritual authority.

And what's most horrifying: it was done in the name of God.

There were no chains. No cages. No guards. But the control was absolute. The fear was real. The trauma was lasting.

This chapter isn't just about one boy—it's about every person who sat in that room and felt powerless. It's about the silence that follows abuse, the confusion that follows manipulation, and the courage it takes to finally name it for what it is.

The Breaking Point – When Silence Was No Longer an Option

After the brutal beating of the seven-year-old boy in front of the congregation, another mother raised her hand. Her son, too, had been acting out in school. She brought the issue before the "Man of God," hoping for guidance. What she received instead was violence.

The boy was about ten years old.

The "Man of God" called him to the front of the church and asked why he was misbehaving.

"I don't know, sir," the boy replied.

That answer wasn't enough.

"Let's see if this belt can help you find out why," the "Man of God" said.

He ordered four men to grab the boy—one on each limb—just as they had done with the first child. Then he summoned the enforcer, the man known only for delivering beatings. And once again, the belt flew.

The boy was beaten until the "Man of God" gave the order to stop. By the end, his back and stomach were covered in lacerations, open wounds, and deep bruises—just like the first boy.

The next day, both boys went to school. Ironically, they attended the same elementary school. At one time, the man of God allowed children to go to public schools, but not for long.

The seven-year-old complained of stomach pain, and his teacher sent him to the nurse. When the nurse asked him to remove his shirt, she was stunned. His back looked like something out of a history book, like the scars of a runaway slave. It was covered in welts, bruises, and open wounds.

She asked him what had happened.

"I was beaten at church," he said.

He also told her he wasn't the only one. He gave the name of the second boy.

The nurse called him in. She asked the same questions and had him remove his shirt. The injuries were identical.

She immediately reported the abuse to DFCS (Department of Family and Children Services), who contacted the Atlanta Police Department. The boys were examined, photographed, and interviewed. Their testimony was clear. Their wounds were undeniable.

Warrants were issued for the arrest of the boys' parents, the "Man of God," and the enforcer.

The children were removed from their homes and placed in state custody. DFCS and the Atlanta Police determined that the boys would not return home until a full investigation was completed.

This was the moment when silence broke. When truth pierced the veil of fear. When the invisible chains began to snap.

It took pain. It took courage. It took the voice of a child and the compassion of a school nurse. But finally, the abuse was exposed.

The Mystery That Backfired – When Evidence Spoke Louder Than Spin

The investigation into the "Man of God" and his congregation didn't just shake the church; it shook the city, the state, and eventually, the nation. It began with two brutally beaten boys, but it didn't end there. The Department of Family and Children Services (DFCS), along with the Atlanta Police Department, launched a full-scale investigation that led to forty-nine children being removed from the homes of members of the House of Prayer church.

The images of children being pulled from their homes were broadcast across local and national media. It was heartbreaking, chaotic, and deeply confusing to the average viewer. Children were kicking, screaming, and fighting tooth and nail to stay with their parents. To many watching, it didn't make sense. Why would abused children fight to stay in an abusive environment?

But that was the brilliance—and the horror—of the "Man of God's" manipulation.

He had instructed every child in the church to resist. "Kick. Fight. Scream. Don't let them take you."

He had members of the congregation purchase video cameras to record the chaos. Those tapes were distributed to news outlets and anyone willing to broadcast them. The footage sent a message across the country —and it worked.

Then came the second part of his plan: change the narrative.

The real issue was child abuse, but the "Man of God" reframed it as a debate over parental rights and corporal punishment. That was the mystery. And it was effective. Suddenly, the conversation shifted. DFCS wasn't seen as protecting children; they were seen as attacking Black families. The question at dinner tables across America became: To spank or not to spank?

Politicians took notice—Rev. Hosea Williams, Billy McKinney, Cynthia McKinney, Tyrone Brooks, Rev. Joseph Lowery, Donzella James. They demanded answers. Why were forty-nine Black children removed from homes with two parents? Why were these families being targeted?

The "Man of God" gained international notoriety. He appeared on CNN, MSNBC, Fox News, and more. He turned DFCS into a national embarrassment. He rallied support from across racial and ideological lines—Black, White, Nation of Islam, even the Ku Klux Klan.

Yes, the KKK reached out to offer their support, agreeing with his stance on corporal punishment. It was surreal. The "Man of God" had found common ground between groups that had never stood on the same side of anything.

But there was one thing he couldn't manipulate: the pictures.

DFCS and the Atlanta Police Department had taken photographs of the boys' backs. Open wounds. Gashes. Blood. Welts.

They looked like they had been whipped by a slave master.

Those images reminded the judge and jury that this wasn't about spanking. This was cruelty. This was abuse. This was criminal.

And those pictures became the "Man of God's" Achilles' heel.

He may have won in the court of public opinion, but in Fulton County Superior Court, where truth mattered more than spin, he lost, mainly because of those pictures of those boys' backs being brutally beaten.

He was sentenced to ten years, serving two years in prison, with the remainder on probation. He left the courtroom a convicted felon and a registered child abuser.

And I knew it. Every member of the congregation knew it.

No mystery could erase those scars.

Don't Go to Sleep While I'm Talking – When Rest Becomes Rebellion

I was thirteen years old.

We were at a Bible study meeting held in one of the member's homes. It wasn't uncommon for the "Man of God's" services to begin at eight in the evening and stretch into the next morning—sometimes until five a.m. That night, we had already been in service for six to eight hours. My body was tired. My mind was exhausted. I began to drift off.

I was seated near the front, close to where the "Man of God" was preaching. He noticed me nodding off and snapped, "You better wake up, or I'm going to put something on your ass."

I knew what that meant. A beating. A belt. A switch.

I jolted awake, trying to stay alert. But it was three in the morning. What normal person wouldn't be sleepy at that hour, especially a thirteen-year-old boy?

Eventually, I couldn't fight it anymore. I fell asleep again.

The next thing I knew, I was being beaten. The "Man of God" was whipping me with a leather belt. It was the worst beating I ever received in my life. Red welts covered my arms, and I'm a dark-skinned person. That's how severe it was.

Years later, something equally disturbing happened.

During another late-night Bible study, the "Man of God's" own wife began to fall asleep. She was exhausted. A thirty-six-year-old woman. The mother of eight children. But instead of compassion, she was met with threats.

"If you don't wake up," he shouted, "I'm going to have the men drag your ass to the back of the church, and your children are going to see your legs in the air and you kicking and screaming!" This statement is very telling to me. It tells me that every time the man of God had someone beaten, or hazed, or ridiculed, that he was aware of the embarrassment it was to your wife, children, and family. It was intentional.

Terrified, she pulled out her cell phone to help herself stay awake. He saw it. He flew into a rage. He snatched the phone from her hands and slammed it to the floor, shattering it.

"When I'm talking, I want your undivided attention!" he roared.

This wasn't leadership. It was tyranny.

This wasn't correction. It was control.

But the Bible tells a different story.

When Jesus was with His disciples in the Garden of Gethsemane, He asked them to stay awake and pray. They fell asleep. He gently asked, "Couldn't you watch with me for one hour?" They fell asleep again. And Jesus said, "Let them sleep."

He understood. He didn't beat them. He didn't threaten them. He didn't shame them.

Because Jesus knew the human body has limits. He knew that rest is not rebellion.

But the "Man of God"? He acted as if he had more authority than Jesus Himself.

This chapter isn't just about sleep. It's about power. It's about fear.

It's about the difference between a shepherd and a tyrant.

Not Even Cold in the Ground – A Marriage That Raised Questions

Before the "Man of God" married his current wife—who is also my biological sister—he had been married to a woman for 43 years. I've spoken of her earlier in this book, and I'll say it again: she was one of the sweetest souls I've ever known. I loved her dearly, and she loved me. When my wife and I first got married, we lived with them for a few months, and she treated us like her own children. Her kindness was genuine, her spirit gentle, and her presence comforting.

She passed away from colon cancer.

Her death was a loss that shook me deeply. I carry precious memories of her—memories that still warm my heart and bring tears to my eyes.

But what happened next left me stunned.

On the very day she was buried, the "Man of God" attempted to marry his new bride, my sister. They weren't able to complete the marriage that day due to missing documents, but just a few days later, it was made official.

His former wife wasn't even cold in the ground.

The marriage was done in secret. Only a select few members of the congregation knew. I—her own brother—had no idea. I didn't know they were dating. I didn't know there were plans. I didn't even know there was a relationship.

And that's what troubled me most.

If they were dating, when did it start? Was his deceased wife still alive when their relationship began? These questions haunted me. My sister later told me she wanted to tell me, but the "Man of God" instructed her not to. I believe he feared my reaction. He knew I would see it as disrespectful, not just to her memory, but to the sacredness of mourning.

Marrying another woman on the same day your wife is buried, it felt wrong. It felt rushed. It felt like her life, her legacy, her love had been swept aside.

It was awkward. It was painful. It was revealing.

This chapter isn't just about a marriage—it's about the erosion of trust. It's about the silence that follows secrets. And it's about the quiet grief of watching someone you loved be replaced before the soil on her grave had settled.

1st Abuse now Child Molestation

My 4-year-old daughter came to me and told her mother and me, that a young man who is a member of the "Man of God's" congregation attempted to molest her. She said that it happened at church one night while the children were outside playing. She said he grabbed her and took her behind a parked car, pulled her dress up, and attempted to pull down her panties. She began to scream and kick, and he let her go. This enraged my wife and me, and I immediately went to the Man of God's house to report what my daughter had revealed. We expected him to deliver some sense of justice for this violation of her innocence. The Man of God called the molester's parents and asked the boy if it was true. They reported back that he denied it, so the Man of God said there was nothing he could do since it was my daughter's word against the boy's.

That's when I began to wonder if the Man of God cared as much about my children and me as he did about his own. By that time, he and my sister had three children together, his biologically, and I knew that if this had been one of his daughters, he would have done far more to uncover the truth. It felt as if he treated the matter as insignificant because these were just Michael's children, expendable. If it had been one of his biological children, that boy would at the very least have been beaten bloody for touching one of his kids, and the matter would have been reported to the authorities.

The molester and his family lived with my wife's sister and her husband at the time. Before this happened, I had warned my wife not to have our children around that family. My protective instincts as a father were alarmed, and I asked her to trust me and heed my warning. She didn't.

By questioning and investigating the matter, we also found out that this same young man had molested my six-year-old and seven-year-old sons as well. My six-year-old son told us that one day, my wife took my children over to her sister's house, where the molester and his family lived, defying what I, her husband, had asked her to do. Not only did she not listen to me, but while my children were over to her sister's house, my son said my wife asked the molester to take two of my boys to the restroom, and that's where he made both of my boys take turns putting his penis in their mouths. Hearing this brought bitter tears to my and my wife's eyes and filled me with rage and anger. We were extremely upset, and we went to the pastor again for justice.

This time, even the man of God had to take the situation seriously, and he addressed the situation openly before the entire congregation. The pastor had the molester's parents question him on the matter. He lied to his parents and denied that anything happened, according to his parents' report. No one believed what he was saying besides his parents and the man of God, so other parents began to suspect that some of their children may have been molested as well. So, after much suspicion and pressure, the child molester eventually admitted to molesting at least 15 children in the house of prayer, including babies amongst the congregation. And what makes matters worse, he admitted it with a smirk on his face. He would literally look at the parents of these children and smirk at them! I, along with some of the other fathers of these molested children, wanted to kill the molester to wipe that smirk right off his face forever

We wanted to immediately report this molester to the authorities for Child Molestation, but the "Man of God" forbade us from reporting it to the Authorities. The "Man of God" said that he does not believe in reporting a church matter to the law because the law is his enemy, and he adamantly insisted that the matter be kept "In-house". I knew that the only reason the man of God said this was because he is a convicted child abuser and served two years in prison and 8 years on probation for Cruelty to Children. However, I strongly doubt if he would be saying this if it were his children who had been molested by this child molester!

Some parents wanted to inflict bodily harm on him.

They were highly upset. Three of my children were molested by this molester, but still, even after all of this, the "Man of God" forbade any of the parents from reporting this to the authorities or carrying out any bodily harm on the molester. He said that the parents did not know how to deal with it and that they would only make a mess out of the situation. The situation was already a mess!! The "Man of God" said he was the only one who knew how to properly deal with the situation. Then the man of God added further insult to injury by suggesting that the molested children were not victims, but they deserved this molestation because of their sins or their parents' sins. He even went as far as sitting the victims down before the congregation and coercing them into confessing what they did to tempt their molester and to repent for doing it. That is, the one's who were old enough to talk because some of the victims were babies less than a year old!

So, the "Man of God" said to the young man, "It seems to me that you like little girls' pussies. So, I am going to arrange for you to marry one of the young women here in the church so you can have you some ‹grown pussy›". Now the molester is married and has two children of his own, and his wife does not trust him with his own children. She is afraid to leave him alone with them. She would take the children with her everywhere she goes because she is afraid that her husband will molest them. She can't even take a bath without taking the children into the bathroom with her. This is the way that the "Man of God" handled the problem. I believe that the "Man of God" did not want this reported because he was afraid of the publicity that would come from this being since he was just convicted of "Cruelty to Children," and now 15 -20 children in his organization were sexually abused by a member of the organization.

Now the Man of God loved publicity, but not this kind of publicity. With the publicity that he received from brutally beating children, he was able to put a spin on it and change the rhetoric from beating children to disciplining children or the right to spank a child, which was almost genius on his part. But with these kids being molested, there was no way he could spin this topic to make himself look good. He was afraid of how it would make him look to the world, which means he didn't care about the well-being of our children, but he cared about his reputation. It would surprise you to know the evil and egregious acts of evil that are covered up with a religious organization. Look at the Catholic church, for example. All the young boys who have been molested by priests, and not one priest has faced criminal charges, because the Catholic Church covers it up.

The "Man of God" and my sister have three biological children. I often wonder if it was their three children that were molested by this Child Molester, would the

"Man of God" have dealt with the matter entirely differently? As a matter of fact, I believe if this child molester had molested any of the "Man of God's" children, he would have first been brutally beaten and then sent to prison a long time ago.

CHAPTER 11
EXODUS AND RETALIATION

My Exodus / Public Enemy #1

This was the time I truly became disenchanted with the "Man of God" and the organization I had been part of, and I knew it was time to leave. My children were precious to me, but it was painfully clear that they were not special to the "Man of God." How could he and his congregation harbor a child molester—a habitual child molester!

My wife, though deeply committed to the "Man of God," disagreed with the way he handled the situation. She drove to the local police station and just sat there crying because she wanted to turn the molester in so badly.

When I decided to report him myself, she vehemently opposed it, out of her devotion to the "Man of God." But I did not let that stop me. I went to the authorities and turned the boy in. I believed it was in the best interest of my children, that for them to recover from being victimized, some measure of justice needed to be delivered. I wanted justice to become a reality for all my children.

After an investigation and media involvement, the molester was sent to jail and later to prison for molesting my three children. He was sentenced to ten years. The sentence could have been far greater if other parents of the 15–20 molested children had had the courage to come forward, but they did not.

From that moment on, I became public enemy number one of the "Man of God" and his congregation. I was the only parent of all those molested children who had the courage to seek justice for my own. I knew that by opposing him, I would have to leave the House of Prayer cult.

The "Man of God" launched a tumultuous campaign of ostracism against me. My wife, my mother, my brother, and other family members who were members of the church joined in. The "Man of God" even sent my mother to my house to try to convince me to return. I told her my mind was made up: I would never go back.

She responded, "Then you are not my son anymore. You are dead to me. You can count me as dead," simply because I left the church. Those words shattered me. I had been very close to my mother, and I loved her dearly. It hurt to have her cut me off so easily.

But I accepted it as the price I had to pay; for my children to receive justice, and for me to reclaim my freedom and my manhood.

The Strength to Leave

For years, I lived in two worlds. One was ruled by fear, control, and rigid doctrine. The other—public school—was messy, imperfect, but full of life. It gave me glimpses of freedom, of possibility, of who I might become.

At school, I learned to think critically. I learned to stand up for myself. I learned that not every authority figure demanded blind obedience. Some wanted me to grow. Some wanted me to succeed. And some—like my elementary school principal and my teachers—wanted me to feel safe.

Those lessons stayed with me. They planted seeds.

I began to notice the cracks in the foundation of the organization I was raised in: the contradictions, the manipulation, the way fear was used to control people, to isolate them, to keep them small. I saw how the "Man of God" demanded loyalty but rarely gave love, how he held people's secrets over their heads like chains, and how he used shame to silence dissent.

And I started asking questions—not out loud at first, but in my heart: Why do I feel so anxious all the time? Why do I have to choose between obedience and dignity? Why does loving God mean losing myself?

The answers didn't come all at once. But the strength did.

It came from every teacher who believed in me. It came from every friend who saw me as more than my circumstances. It came from every moment I stood up to a bully and refused to back down.

Eventually, I realized I didn't have to stay. I didn't have to keep living in fear. I didn't have to keep pretending that silence was holiness.

Leaving wasn't easy. It meant walking away from everything I'd ever known. It meant risking relationships, reputation, and security. But it also meant choosing truth. Choosing healing. Choosing myself.

And that choice—however long it took to make—was the beginning of freedom.

When I decided to leave the House of Prayer, I just wanted us to go our separate ways: they theirs, me mine. I still wanted to stay married and be a devoted father to our twelve children, as I had been for eighteen years. But the "Man of God" made it clear he believed my family belonged to him, and that he had absolute control over my wife and kids.

My wife continued attending the church against my

wishes and kept taking the children there, giving the "Man of God" direct contact with them. He and my wife began instructing the children on how to disrupt our home because I had broken fellowship with his leadership and congregation. Their first objective was to strip me of authority, respect, and affection in my own house.

They fed my children poisonous rhetoric. They said things like, "Your daddy is a nasty ass pussy licker, and he may have eaten shit too," referring to an incident from when I was five years old, which happened at least thirty years earlier. They spoke of it as if it had just happened yesterday. My wife would call me names in front of the children, "nigger" or "trashy ass nigger." She began sending the children places without telling me where they were. When I asked, "Where are the children?" she replied, "Nigger, none of your business."

One evening, she left the house, and I had no idea where she'd gone. All the children were home with me. Later that same night, our fifteen-year-old daughter slipped out and jumped into a car with a married man from the church. His wife was not in the car. When I found out, I had him bring her back. I reprimanded her for leaving without my permission, and she was defiant, telling me she did not need my permission if the "Man of God" had given her permission.

I warned her that if she did it again, she would get a whipping. She told her mother, and when my wife came home, she warned me that neither she nor the children had to tell me anything because I was no longer under the "Man of God's" teachings and was in conflict with him. She threatened that if I tried to discipline any of the children, she would "have my ass locked up."

I told her I was her husband and the father of our children, and that God had placed me as the head of our household. She shot back, "No, you are not the head of this household. The 'Man of God' is the head of this household." I was only trying to protect our daughter, yet I was being threatened with jail for doing it.

One day, I decided to take my children to the mall. We did this often, and it was something we all enjoyed. I loaded everyone into our sixteen-passenger van, and we headed to Cumberland Mall. We went shopping, then stopped at the food court, where everyone ate wherever they wanted. We laughed, talked, and had a great time together.

When we got back in the van and headed home, I felt thankful for the day we had shared. But when we arrived, their mother immediately called the "Man of God" to tell him I had taken the children to the mall.

Now, what I'm about to share, I didn't find out until much later. And honestly, that was a blessing. To this day, I thank God I didn't know at the time—because I don't know what I might have done.

At the next church meeting, the "Man of God" chastised my children and excommunicated them for going to the mall with their daddy. He announced to the congregation, including our relatives, that no one was to speak to any of my children for a period of time. It was his way of punishing me for leaving the church and trying to rob me of the natural affection between my children and me.

My children told me about it long after it happened. They said it was one of the hardest things they'd ever gone through—how much it hurt that even their grandparents, cousins, and close friends refused to talk to them. By then, he had already turned my wife and mother against me, and now he was trying to make my children turn against me too.

The "Man of God" was determined to use every resource at his disposal to destroy me. I had become public enemy number one of the House of Prayer and its leader, Reverend Arthur Allen Jr.

It is hard to be the man of your house with a constant threat like that hanging over your head, but I was determined to remain. Every chance my wife got, she reminded me—sometimes daily—how she would "have my ass locked up" if I disciplined any of our children in any way.

The irony of this still amazes me. The same "Man of God" she was devoted to was a convicted felon who had served prison time for having children brutally beaten until they were bruised and bloody. I had never abused any of my children. This wasn't about caring for the well-being of a child; it was about stripping me of respect and authority in my own home. The "Man of God" believed that if you weren't under his authority, he had the right to take away yours.

For some reason, he took a particular interest in my oldest daughter. She, along with my wife, became his main weapon of manipulation. He used them to hurt me, to provoke me, to push me toward either returning to his leadership or doing something I would regret.

The "Man of God" wanted me to crawl back to him on my hands and knees, begging to be restored to his good graces and to the approval of the congregation. That way, he could end the psychological games he was playing through my family and appear merciful for doing so. His other plan was to push me so far that I would lash out violently against my family, giving him the perfect reason to have me arrested. Either outcome would have been a victory for him.

But my mind was made up. I was going to stand my ground and never go back to the "Man of God's" congregation.

During this time, my feelings were dark. I battled violent thoughts toward him because of the games he was playing with my family—people who meant everything to me. I knew he was putting his health and well-being on the line by provoking me like that. I used to imagine ways I could hurt him, but deep down I knew that doing so would only play into his hands. That awareness was the only thing keeping me from making a mistake I couldn't take back.

This was what made the "Man of God" so dangerous. He would have loved for me to assault him, to give him the chance to make good on my wife's threats to "have my ass locked up." Tampering with my family was a dangerous game for him, but I knew I had to exercise restraint. I was aware of how conniving he was, and I understood that his goal was to push me until I lost control.

He was confident that he held the upper hand. And honestly, without God on my side, he did. The man was not large in stature; he was skinny and old, but his ability to manipulate people was unmatched. He also had life experience I didn't have. I had been raised in the cult, sheltered from the world, naïve to many of the tricks I was now facing.

He had the years, the experience, and the words that could twist reality itself. And for so long, I was exactly what he needed—a believer, sheltered and naïve, easy to mold. But now, I see beyond his tricks. The world is bigger than the one he built for me, and I am no longer trapped inside it. He may remain in his own illusion, but I walk freely into my truth.

The "Man of God" then began to employ a tactic in my home that I had never encountered before. Although I was no longer a member of his congregation, I remained committed to my home, my wife, and our children. Throughout our entire marriage, I had been faithful—she was the only woman I shared intimacy with. Despite my natural desires as a man, I never strayed.

However, in an effort to disrupt any affection between us, the Man of God instructed my wife to read scripture aloud whenever I initiated intimacy. She followed his guidance precisely. It was strange, even unsettling, but she was the only woman I had, and so I accepted it. Through it all, I remained true and devoted.

A couple of months passed, and I was still standing my ground, refusing to return to the Man of God's congregation. He then decided to escalate his attack. On Sunday morning, July 10th, 2011, after my wife had taken my children to an almost all-night meeting the night before, I awoke to the sounds of my oldest daughter moving through the house, ranting and shouting that she didn't have a daddy. She claimed she wished she had a daddy like the Man of God and, as a matter of fact, that he was more of a daddy to her than I was. It was obvious she was performing this tempestuous display to make me hear her.

In that moment, I became extremely angry. I knew

the Man of God had coached my daughter to do this, to turn my children against me. My wife was planning to take the children to his church that day, but I refused. I told her she could go, but my children would not be going with her. I forbade it.

Knowing my wife would likely ignore me, I decided to disable the family van she normally drove to church. Shortly after, I received a call from a customer needing their air conditioning fixed, so I took a shower and prepared to go to work. By the time I got out, my wife and children were gone. I looked outside and noticed our car, a small four-door sedan that could seat only six passengers at most, was gone. I knew there was no way she could have packed all 13 of them in that car, but I knew they were headed to church.

I hopped in my work van to intercept them. Along the way, I saw about four of my children walking, so I stopped and had them get in the van with me. As I continued toward the church, I saw my wife driving ahead. I followed her, but once she noticed me, she began fleeing in a direction away from the church. I tried to wave her down, signaling for her to stop so I could get my children, but she refused. Eventually, I stopped following her and returned home with the four children I had picked up, then went on to work.

Later, at the job site, I received a call from an Atlanta police officer. My wife had reported that I tried to run her and the kids off the road. I told the officer this was not true and explained exactly what had happened.

Fortunately for me, the Atlanta Police Department was very familiar with the Man of God and his congregation and was aware of his fanatical, cult-like practices. They almost immediately understood my plight. The department had previously intervened in the Man of God's organization a few years earlier, removing 49 children after two boys were beaten in a ritualistic fashion by a group of five men, so they were well acquainted with his tactics.

I decided to stay in a hotel that night to allow things to cool off between my wife and me, returning home the next day. At the time, I was in the middle of converting my garage into a children's playroom for my kids, so I continued working on the project. By the end of the day, as I was finishing up, I heard a knock at the door. When I answered, it was a Fulton County Sheriff's deputy. I was served with divorce papers and a restraining order, alleging that I had attempted to harm my wife and children by trying to run them off the road.

I protested my innocence to the deputy, but it was to no avail. The deputy informed me that until the court hearing, which was thirty days away, I had to turn over my house keys and leave. If I came within 500 yards of my wife or children before the hearing, I would be in violation of the restraining order and immediately taken to jail.

I turned over my keys and walked out. On my way out, I turned to my wife and asked, "Is this what you want, or is it what the Man of God wants?" She responded, "It's what I want! If you don't want to be a member of the Man of God's congregation, then I don't want you!"

I had been a member of the Man of God's congregation for over thirty years, ever since I was four, and I knew for certain that neither my wife nor any member would make a decision of this magnitude without the direct instruction of the Man of God. Members couldn't even decide to buy a car, purchase a house, or go on vacation without his permission, so how much more for a woman with twelve children to divorce her husband?

The Bible says the only justifiable cause for divorce is adultery or fornication. I was guilty of neither, meaning my wife had no biblical cause to file for divorce. The Man of God was the one instructing her to do so, directly opposing the Word of God. Does the Man of God have the right to instruct his members to disobey scripture?

So, I was homeless—losing my wife and family—and I had no one to turn to. This is the danger of cutting off all your relatives and family outside of the congregation. I was devastated. I was in the middle of a storm, feeling powerless over my direction and my outcome. I knew the Man of God was far more cunning and crafty than I was, but I also knew someone had to take a stand against him, because what he was doing was wrong.

The Man of God knew exactly how to manipulate the system, and he had already begun using it against me. I was now facing divorce, along with a temporary restraining order. It felt as if every possible odd was stacked against me.

I thought about African Americans during the height of the civil rights movement and the impossible odds they faced while trying to change this nation. They had to be almost insane to believe that a group of poor Black men and women—with no money, no weapons (because they chose to fight nonviolently), and no political power —could challenge the system that White America was determined to preserve. But they trusted in the power of God through Christ Jesus. Only a people of faith that strong, that "crazy," could put their lives on the line and still believe God would give them victory.

My twelve children were being held captive by the Man of God, and he was using my wife as a weapon against me. Even though everything seemed to be against me, I made up my mind to put my faith in God through Christ Jesus. I believed He would help me rescue my children and myself from this situation.

I found a small hotel in downtown Atlanta that offered a decent monthly rate. I spoke with the manager, explained my situation, and he agreed to work with me. Even though I had been put out of my home, I still had to pay all the household bills—and now I had to take care of myself too. How could I possibly support a wife and twelve children in one house and also survive on my own in another? I didn't make much money, and I was deeply worried and afraid.

For the first time in my life, I felt like giving up. But something near that hotel kept me from doing it. Right across the street was a huge homeless shelter, surrounded by people who practically lived on the side-walks. I imagined the shelter was too full to take everyone in, so some had no choice but to stay outside. I passed by them every day—mostly men—sleeping on hard concrete, sometimes in terrible weather, yet somehow content.

Watching them stirred something in me. I realized that some of these men might have faced situations like mine—broken families, betrayal, despair—and it had crushed them. I felt deep empathy for them, because I knew I could easily end up the same way if I stopped fighting. I wasn't just fighting for my family—I was fighting for my life.

Then the Holy Spirit began to speak to me, reminding me of how Jesus fed five thousand people with two fish and five loaves of bread. If He could perform a miracle like that, then surely He could make a way for me to feed my family and myself. After all, we were only fourteen people—nowhere near five thousand. So I heard God telling me, "Be of good cheer, and be not afraid, for I am with you."

Legal Representation

I decided to seek legal representation for my divorce and my TPO hearing, or restraining order. I went online and found a firm in Atlanta known for representing men in divorce cases. I had a consultation with an attorney from the firm, explained my situation, and told him that my wife of nineteen years had filed for divorce and that we had twelve children together. I also informed him about the "Man of God" and his involvement in the situation.

Immediately, the attorney said he was familiar with the "Man of God's" organization because of prior cases with Fulton County DFCS and the Atlanta Police Department. Then he asked me a question that stopped me in my tracks:

"I know your wife filed for divorce, but do you really want this divorce to go through?"

I was taken aback. "What do you mean? Do I have a choice? She's the one filing for divorce," I replied.

The attorney explained, "You are correct—she filed for divorce. But I have seen situations just like yours. The wife will file, put the husband through a year or two of hell, and then, at the final divorce hearing, she may tell the judge she's changed her mind and no longer wants the divorce. The reason? To extend the time she can put you through more hell. If the person who filed decides they no longer want the divorce, the judge will dismiss the case. So I'm asking: do you want this divorce to go through?"

This was not an easy question. I had never considered the possibility that the divorce could be dismissed, even after all we had endured. It meant something to me that it was my wife who filed, not me. Despite everything she and the "Man of God" had put me through, if it were left up to me, I would never have filed for divorce. I would have endured it all to stay with her and our children.

I took a long moment to think. Over the years, I had hoped her sentiment toward me would change, but she consistently made it clear that it had not. Finally, I reached a point where I realized: if she didn't want me, then I didn't want her.

I looked at the attorney and said, "Yes, I do want the divorce to go through."

He responded, "Then the first thing we have to do is file a counterclaim for divorce on your behalf. This will protect you if your wife decides to change her mind at the final hearing and sees things not going the way she expected."

I nodded. "If you think this is best, then file the counterclaim."

Little did I know at the time how this legal action would prove prophetic and pivotal in securing a positive outcome at the final divorce hearing, which you will see as you continue reading.

The next thing the lawyer wanted to discuss was the cost of representation. The initial retainer fee was $3,000, and it would be approximately $3,000 per month until my divorce was finalized. I honestly did not see how I was going to be able to pay $3,000 per month, but I was able to cover the initial retainer, so I paid it and now had legal counsel.

Initially, when I was served divorce papers, my wife requested joint custody of the children. I was okay with that under a few conditions. My number one condition was that my children were never to be around the child molester once he was released from prison. The "Man of God" had all the parents in the congregation remove their children from public schools and required them to be homeschooled so that no teacher or school official could report further abuse if another child was brutally beaten. This so-called homeschooling was nothing but a sham. Seventy-five percent of the congregation had not finished high school, and only one member held a college degree. Who was going to properly educate these children?

According to state progress reports, many children in the "Man of God's" congregation were so far behind academically that twelve- and thirteen-year-olds were performing at second- or third-grade levels. I wanted all of my children to have a mainstream education, so another condition was that they be placed in public schools.

My third condition was that none of my children would marry before the age of eighteen. I did not want my daughters forced into marriage at fourteen or fifteen, having multiple children before they were mature enough to decide for themselves if they wanted that lifestyle. I wanted my children to grow up with the mindset that "the sky is the limit." In the "Man of God's" congregation, the highest aspiration for a girl was to become a wife and mother of multiple children. I'm not saying there's anything wrong with that, but I wanted my daughters to have all options available to them. It is 2020, and we have just elected our first female Vice President, a woman of color. It is only a matter of time before we have our first female President of the United States, and I want that option available to my girls as well.

My fourth condition was that my children receive no corporal punishment or ritualistic beatings from anyone. The Fulton County judicial system and the Atlanta Police Department were well aware of the "Man of God" and his congregation because of their radical belief in beating children until they were bloody and scarred. He had been convicted of "Cruelty to Children" and sentenced to ten years in prison.

With these conditions in mind, my lawyer prepared to request them at our first divorce hearing.

Before our first divorce hearing, I had to attend the Restraining Order (TPO) hearing, which took place on August 5, 2011. My lawyer did not attend because he felt that the judge would immediately see there was no just cause to uphold it and would rule in my favor. Additionally, attending the hearing would have meant paying hourly fees I could not afford, so we decided to save those hours for the divorce hearing scheduled a week later.

When I appeared before the judge, a white woman in the Fulton County Superior Court, I explained that my wife and I had twelve children and had been married for nineteen years. I also informed her that we were both members of the "House of Prayer Cult" congregation and described how 15 to 20 children in the congregation had been molested by a member, including three of my own children. I explained that the "Man of God" did not want to report the abuse to the authorities, which was why I left the organization and reported the matter to ensure some sense of justice for my children.

Because of this, the "Man of God" had instructed my

wife to file for divorce and abuse the legal system by filing a restraining order against me based on false claims, which led to my eviction from our home.

The judge then allowed my wife to present her case. She had no legal representation and spoke on her own behalf. The judge asked, "How did your husband attempt to harm you, ma'am?" She responded, "Well, he didn't attempt to harm me, but he was following me in my car, and he caused me to run off the road."

The judge pressed, "So he ran you off the road?"

She replied, "No, he didn't run me off the road, but he caused me to."

The judge asked, "How did he cause you to run off the road?"

She answered, "Because he was following me."

The judge then turned to me: "Mr. Oglesby, what does she mean that you caused her to run off the road?"

I explained, "Your Honor, I don't know what she means. I was following her because I did not want my children returning to the cult she still attends. The leader of the cult was feeding my children untrue and poisonous rhetoric to alienate them from me and create confusion and chaos in my home, all because I decided to leave the organization."

The judge then addressed my wife directly: "Ma'am, this court deals with a lot of serious domestic violence cases, and you are wasting the court's time by attempting to abuse the system to gain an advantage in a pending divorce case. You want a divorce, which is your right, but you should have simply filed for divorce."

The judge chastised her, warned her not to misuse the legal system in this manner again, and dismissed the case.

The judge went a step further and issued a visitation order allowing me to be with my children every other weekend. She asked if I intended to move back into the house, since technically, with the restraining order dismissed, I could return. I told her that I had no intention of moving back, as my wife had already filed for divorce.

The judge stipulated that every other Friday at 6:00 p.m., my wife had to vacate the house so I could stay there with the children until Sunday at 6:00 p.m., when she could return. This was a very unusual visitation order, one I had never encountered before. It was clear that the judge recognized how my wife and the "Man of God" were trying to destroy my relationship with my children. Her order reflected both her disapproval of their actions and her support for me.

The judge wanted me to begin visitations that very week. A couple of days later, on Friday at 6:00 p.m., I went to the house to move in with my children. The problem was that my wife disobeyed the judge and refused to leave. I reminded her of the judge's order: she was to leave and return Sunday at 6:00 p.m.

She responded, "I don't care what the judge said! I am not leaving my kids in the house alone with a 'trashy ass nigger' like you!"

This is what happens when you leave a cult: you are demonized and ostracized. In this congregation, it went to an entirely new level. To them, I was no more than a "trashy ass nigger." I had cared for my wife and our children for nineteen years, remained faithful to her, never abused her, and provided well for our family. None of that mattered anymore, because I was no longer a member of the "Man of God's" cult.

So, I moved in anyway with the kids. She allowed me to have the main bedroom while she slept in another room. Although it was very awkward, I was still glad to be with my children and looked forward to spending the weekend with them.

I gathered all my kids in the living room to have a conversation about my intentions toward them. They asked, "Daddy, why have you abandoned us?" I told them, "I have not abandoned you. I am not the one who filed for divorce. The Man of God instructed your mother to do this because I am no longer a member of his congregation. I will never abandon you. In fact, I am going to make sure you all have great futures ahead of you. I plan to help each of you build successful lives."

I began to speak life over them, telling them about the plans I had for their growth, like trees that would blossom and grow tall. I explained that I would place them in the right environment, ensuring they received an education above a sixth-grade homeschooling level and giving them the freedom to choose their own paths in life. This vision for my children was contrary to the Man of God's plan, but God had given them to me. "I love all of you with all my heart," I told them, "and I will be there for you until my last breath."

Already, the Man of God and my wife were trying to paint a false narrative in my children's minds that I had abandoned them, but I refused to let that take root. I told my kids that the next day we would go out and have a great time together that weekend. I then went to my quarters, separate from my wife, who still refused to leave as the judge had ordered, and went to sleep for the evening.

The next morning, I awoke excited to spend the day with my kids—but my wife had a surprise for me. All the children were gone. She had taken them away early to disrupt my visitation. I found myself in a real-life "War of the Roses" situation—a reference to the movie about a couple who, during their divorce, stayed in the same house, leading to chaos and near violence. I was not intent on going through that, so I decided to leave the house and inform the judge at our next hearing, seeking permission to take my children with me on my next visitation.

From the beginning, my wife made her disdain for the courts and disrespect for authority evident. This trait, she inherited from the Man of God, who was famous for defying the law and the authority of the court system. He believed that, as "The Man of God," his authority superseded that of any earthly legal system. After all, he represented God himself, so he answered only to Him.

But the Bible teaches that we are to recognize the laws of the land and respect those in authority, unless their demands conflict with God's Word. This mystique of the Man of God—the way he boldly defied judges—kept his congregation in awe. When he was convicted of cruelty to children and sentenced to ten years, he was initially ordered to serve only thirty days in jail with the rest on probation. However, he refused to obey the probation terms and was subsequently ordered to serve two years.

This same defiant trait had been passed down to my wife, and, in this case, it wound up working to my advantage.

Judges do not like being disobeyed, but my wife seemed to enjoy telling them what she would and would not do. I couldn't believe how, throughout our divorce process, she defied one judge after another.

When we arrived at our first divorce hearing, I was anxious for my lawyer to present my conditions for joint custody. My goal was for my wife to have physical custody of the children while ensuring that I maintained my rights as a father, and to make the judge aware of how she had disobeyed the visitation order issued at the restraining order hearing.

My lawyer presented all my conditions professionally, and they sounded reasonable to the judge. The judge then turned to my wife and asked if she would abide by them.

That's when she dropped a bombshell: "I have decided that I don't want joint custody with him. I want full custody, and he can have supervised visitations."

This hit me hard. It completely changed the situation. I realized she was trying to keep me out of my children's lives forever. She wasn't trying to share custody or tie the game—she was going for the knockout.

The judge, sensing the gravity of the situation, asked my wife, "Why would you not want to share custody with the children's father?"

She responded, "Because he said that if he wasn't a member of the 'Man of God's" congregation, that he would fuck his own daughter! Well, he is no longer a member of the "Man of God's" congregation, so according to what he said, I believe he will try to have sex with his daughters." The judge turned to me and asked, “Mr. Oglesby, is this true what your wife is saying?” I told the Judge, “No, your honor, she is lying. My Mother said that her daddy, who is my grandfather, molested her as a girl. My brother’s daughter told me that my brother attempted to molest her. What I said to my wife and all the “Man of God’s” congregation was that I thank God that I was not like my Grandfather or my brother because I would never attempt to have sex with any of my children. It was a testimony I gave before the entire congregation of the “Man of God,” one that she is now twisting in court completely out of context. This is just another attempt to demonize and scandalize me because I am no longer part of the “Man of God’s” cult.”

The judge said, “I believe you, Mr. Oglesby, because I’ve heard of these kinds of things being talked about during the ‘Man of God’s’ church services. However, she does have the right to ask for full custody of the children, and I cannot, by law, force her to change her request.” The judge then ordered us to attend mediation before our next scheduled hearing.

Before we left, I told the judge about the visitation arrangement that had been ordered by another judge during the restraining order hearing that was later dismissed. I explained how my wife disobeyed that order, how she refused to leave the house as instructed, and then took all the children away the very next day to disrupt my visit. The judge turned to her and asked, "Is this true?"

She replied, "I was not going to leave my children at the house with somebody like him! He's not a member of the church anymore, and I don't know what he might do to my kids!"

The judge then looked at me and asked if I was able to take the kids with me during my next scheduled visit. "Yes, your honor, I can do that," I answered. The judge then verbally reprimanded my wife for disobeying a court order and gave her a stern warning not to interfere with any future visits, or there would be dire consequences.

When my lawyer and I left the courtroom, I broke down in tears. I cried because I didn't want to believe that my wife and the "Man of God" would stoop to such low levels. That may sound strange, but even with all our differences, I still wanted to believe they wouldn't resort to outright lies.

When she first filed for divorce, her papers requested joint custody of the children. So why now was she suddenly asking for full custody—with supervised visitations? This had the "Man of God's" name written all over it. I knew that every move my wife made against me was guided by him, though she was also a willing participant. I knew who the puppet was—and who the Puppet Master was.

The "Man of God" and my wife were playing for keeps. They were determined to take my kids and leave me with nothing. If they had succeeded, it would have destroyed me. At that moment, I realized I had to be just as determined as they were. I would have to fight for full custody myself.

They were feeding my children poisonous lies, and if I didn't get them out of that cult, their lives would be ruined—and they would grow to hate me. I couldn't live with that. My life was on the line, and my kids were being held hostage in a world of manipulation and fear. I was their only hope for rescue.

I consulted with my lawyer and told him that I now wanted to seek full physical and legal custody of my kids. He shook his head and said he wouldn't advise it because it was very unlikely that any judge would take twelve children from their mother and give them to their father.

"You're financially bleeding right now," he said. "You need to focus on stopping that bleeding. But if you want to try for custody, I'll represent you—it's just going to be expensive."

"How expensive?" I asked.

"It could cost as much as fifty thousand dollars for me to represent you in a full custody case," he replied. "And honestly, I doubt you could win."

Then he added, "After today, your balance is negative three thousand dollars."

I looked at him in disbelief. "Are you saying that the first three thousand I paid you is gone, and now I owe you another three thousand, so a total of six thousand?"

"Yes, that's correct," he said.

I told him, "The only thing you've done for me besides showing up in court today is file a counterclaim for divorce on my behalf."

"Yes, I'm aware," he said, "but those things required a lot of hours, and we charge by the hour."

So I paid the remaining three thousand dollars, but I also told him I could no longer afford his services and had to let him go. He had become part of my "financial bleeding," the very thing he'd warned me to stop. At least, that's how I felt at the time. But as it turned out, the six thousand dollars I spent on that lawyer was worth every penny.

Now I was in search of not just affordable legal representation, but someone who believed in my cause, a lawyer willing to take on the colossal task of convincing a judge to take twelve children from their mother and give them to me, their father.

I went to see another prominent attorney in Atlanta for a consultation. I explained my situation, and he was already familiar with the "Man of God's" congregation and their history with the Atlanta Police Department and Fulton County DFCS.

"Let me tell you right now," he said, "there isn't a judge in Georgia who will take twelve children from a mother and give them to you. There's no chance that will happen. My advice is to work out a deal with your wife that you both can live with. I'll help you do that—but you may as well forget about getting custody. It's not going to happen. My retainer fee is five thousand dollars. I accept checks, cash, or credit cards."

I looked at him and said, "Thank you, counselor, for your time, but I'll pass. I need a lawyer who believes in my cause."

I knew it was a long shot, but I truly believed that if I could stand before a judge and explain how three of my children had been molested by a member of that cult—how my wife insisted on keeping them there, how the leader wanted to cover it up, and how my children were being deprived educationally—the truth would matter. I couldn't stand by and watch my seven daughters risk being forced into arranged marriages at fourteen years old.

The constant attempts by my wife and the cult leader to alienate my children's love for me had gone too far. I believed I had a strong case. So I decided to put my trust in God and move forward with my mission. Even if I had to represent myself, my case would be heard. And if I failed, at least I would know I did everything in my power to rescue my kids and give them a chance at the life they deserved.

I knew I had a steep hill to climb—but I was ready to climb it.

I don't know how it is in the North, but here in the South, when a man and woman are going through a divorce, it seems the woman has all the power. The system is set up in her favor, designed to protect her more than the man. I found this out the hard way at our next hearing.

I arrived at court with no legal representation because, frankly, I couldn't afford one. I also couldn't qualify for free representation through Legal Aid since my wife was already being represented by one of their attorneys, which created a conflict of interest. So there I was, standing alone before the court, while my wife came in with a young white female attorney by her side.

Her lawyer asked the court to grant temporary custody of the children to my wife until the final divorce hearing. She also requested that I continue paying the household bills and cover any legal fees my wife might incur during the process.

The judge turned to me and asked, "Do you have any objections to these terms?"

I replied, "No, Your Honor, I don't object."

The judge then ordered me to pay $2,400 a month in

child support, including all of the household bills, as well as any legal fees my wife might accrue.

You could see the satisfaction on my wife's face. To her, this was a victory—a checkmate. I could almost hear her thinking that this ruling would mark the beginning of my downfall. They believed there was no way I could sustain paying $2,400 each month while also covering my own living expenses. They thought I would eventually break down and come crawling back to the "Man of God" on my hands and knees.

But I saw it differently. That day's ruling didn't hurt me—it helped me.

First, I had faith that God would provide the finances I needed to meet my obligations. I had been taking care of my family for nineteen years, and I wasn't afraid of that responsibility. Second, I knew that proving I could financially support my twelve children would help me in the long run. When the courts saw that I was capable and consistent, it would strengthen my case for custody. So I left that hearing feeling at peace with the decision.

Another thing I knew was that the Fulton County Court system was well aware of Arthur Allen Jr. and the House of Prayer cult. I saw this as an opportunity to start planting the seeds of my case with the judge.

A Father's Stand: Faith, Justice, and the Fight for My Children

Then the judge asked if I had anything to say. I did.

I told the court that three of my children had been molested by a member of the House of Prayer, the place my wife and I had belonged to since childhood. I explained that the leader, Arthur Allen Jr., chose to protect the abuser rather than seek justice. I had turned the molester in, against the wishes of Allen and my wife. In retaliation, Allen instructed my wife to file for divorce and to seek a restraining order based on false charges. She obeyed. I was evicted from my home.

I told the judge that my children were being neglected educationally and emotionally, and that my seven daughters were at risk of being forced into arranged marriages as young as fourteen, just as my wife and I had been. I said, "Your Honor, I will be seeking full custody of all my children."

The judge listened. He acknowledged familiarity with Arthur Allen Jr. and the House of Prayer. He ordered a guardian ad litem to investigate my claims and to represent the children's interests. That moment was a turning point.

As we left the courtroom, my wife and her supporters celebrated their perceived victory. But I knew better. The court was not focused on me or her; it was focused on the children. I had just shown the court who was truly fighting for them.

There is a story in the Bible about two women who claimed the same child. King Solomon proposed cutting the baby in half to settle the dispute. One woman agreed. The other, the true mother, begged the king to spare the child even if it meant giving him up. Solomon knew then who the real parent was.

I am that parent. I will not let my children be divided, manipulated, or sacrificed. I will fight with faith, with truth, and with love.

The judge responded, "I understand, Mr. Oglesby. I am familiar with Pastor Arthur Allen Jr. and his organization. However, that will have to be determined at a future hearing, after you and your wife have completed mediation. In the meantime, the court will assign a Guardian ad Litem to represent the children and investigate the concerns you've brought to the court's attention today."

As we exited the courtroom, several members of the House of Prayer were waiting in the hallway. My wife was celebrating what she believed was her victory—being awarded $2,400 a month—and her supporters joined in her celebration. But I knew they were focused on the wrong thing. Even though I had to pay that steep amount each month, I felt I had planted the seeds of victory in court that day.

PART IV
BREAKING AWAY AND REBUILDING

CHAPTER 12
HEALING AFTER THE CULT

The Plate That Spoiled – Healing Beyond the Dress Code

About a year after I left the House of Prayer cult, I received a phone call from my cousin. She told me that her sister—also my cousin—had finally left the cult, too. I was stunned. She was one of the young girls the "Man of God" had arranged to marry at just 14 years old. The man she married was well into his twenties.

By the time she left, she was around 30 years old and had nine children.

She had never known what it meant to be a normal teenage girl. By 15, she was already a wife and a mother. I knew she would need support. And honestly, I needed her too. We were both survivors—trying to rebuild lives shaped by control, fear, and silence.

About a week after she left the organization, she called me. We talked for a long time. I reassured her that she was going to be okay. I told her that if she ever needed anything, I'd be there. She has an extraordinary story, and I hope one day she writes her own book. I want to hear it—from her perspective. From the eyes of a 14-year-old girl seduced into an arranged marriage and forced into motherhood before she could even finish growing up.

One night, she called and told me she had cooked dinner and made a plate for me. She asked if I'd come by and pick it up. I was thrilled. After weeks of fast food and loneliness, the thought of a home-cooked meal made me feel cared for—seen.

I arrived at her house, knocked on the door, and she opened it with a warm smile. I was happy to see her. She was happy to see me.

But then I froze.

She was wearing pants.

It was the first time I had ever seen her in anything other than the long, floor-sweeping dresses mandated by the House of Prayer. And I was traumatized. I tried to hide it, but she later told me she could see the discomfort all over my face.

I felt sick.

She handed me the plate, and I thanked her. But when I got back to my hotel room, I couldn't eat. I put the plate in the refrigerator, and that's where it stayed—until it spoiled.

For years, I had been taught that any woman who wore pants was a whore or a slut. That teaching was so deeply engraved in my soul that a simple act of kindness—a plate of food from someone I loved—was overshadowed by a pair of pants.

That night showed me how deep the indoctrination ran. How much healing I still had to do. How much unlearning was ahead of me.

But I also knew this: I wasn't going to let it keep me from my cousin. She mattered too much. Her freedom mattered too much. And so did mine.

At the time, I was paying around $550 a month for my hotel room. I decided to ask my cousin if I could move in with her for the same amount each month. That way, the money could go to her instead of the hotel. It would help both of us—she'd have extra support, and I wouldn't have to face my healing journey alone.

Unlearning the Chains – Rebuilding After the Cult

That night with my cousin—the plate of food I couldn't eat, the pants I couldn't unsee—became a turning point.

It revealed that even after leaving the House of Prayer cult, its teachings were still living inside me. Not in my beliefs, but in my reactions. In my discomfort. In my silence.

For years, I had lived under the rule of a man who taught that a woman in pants was a woman without virtue. That modesty was measured by fabric length, not by character. That control was holiness. And even though I had walked away from the cult physically, I hadn't yet walked away emotionally.

But I wanted to.

I wanted to be free—not just from the building, but from the mindset. From fear. From judgment. And my cousin, in her quiet courage, helped me begin that process.

She had left behind everything she knew. She stepped into a world she had never been allowed to explore, with nine children, no roadmap, and a heart full of hope. If she could do that, I could face my own healing.

We began to rebuild our relationship slowly and honestly. We talked about the past, about the teachings, about the lies we'd been fed. We laughed. We cried. We challenged each other. And through those conversations, I started to feel the chains loosen.

I began to question everything I had been taught.

Why did clothing define morality? Why did silence equal submission? Why did fear masquerade as faith?

The answers didn't come all at once. But asking the questions was a start.

I started reading scripture for myself—not through the lens of control, but through the lens of grace. I began listening to voices outside the cult—people who spoke about freedom, love, and truth. I started reclaiming my own voice.

And I began to see my cousin not as a symbol of rebellion, but as a symbol of resilience.

She wasn't just wearing pants. She was wearing freedom.

And I was learning to celebrate it.

Faith After the Fire – Reclaiming God Beyond the Cult

Leaving the House of Prayer cult was like stepping out of a burning building. I was scorched, shaken, and unsure of what was left. But I was alive. And for the first time in years, I could breathe.

But breathing wasn't the same as believing.

I had to start over—not just with my relationships, my identity, and my healing—but with my faith. The version of God I had been taught was rigid, angry, and obsessed with punishment. He was a God who watched every move, waiting to strike. A God who spoke only through one man. A God who demanded obedience but rarely offered comfort.

I couldn't follow that God anymore.

So, I began to search.

I read scripture—not to reinforce old doctrines, but to discover new truths. I found Jesus again—not the one used to justify beatings and control, but the one who sat with sinners, wept with mourners, and forgave without conditions.

I began listening to voices outside the cult—pastors, teachers, thinkers—people who spoke of grace, of love, of freedom. I didn't agree with everything I heard, but I didn't have to. That was the beauty of it. Faith was no longer a cage—it was a conversation.

I prayed differently. Not out of fear, but out of longing. I asked questions. I wrestled with doubt. I allowed myself to be honest with God, even when I was angry, confused, or numb.

And slowly, something began to shift.

I stopped seeing God as a tyrant and started seeing Him as a father. A healer. A companion. I stopped measuring my worth by how well I followed rules and started embracing the truth that I was loved—even in my brokenness.

Redefining my faith didn't happen overnight. It was messy. It was painful. It was sacred.

But it was mine.

And for the first time, I wasn't following a man. I was following God.

The Unexpected Light – Healing in the Haze

By the time the dust began to settle—from courtroom battles, public scandal, and the slow unraveling of my marriage—I had picked up an addiction. One that drained my wallet and clouded my spirit.

I became addicted to strip clubs.

Before the divorce, I had never stepped foot in one. But curiosity, loneliness, and lust became a dangerous cocktail. I wasn't chasing pleasure; I was chasing distraction. I was trying to escape the silence of an empty home, the ache of betrayal, and the weight of being misunderstood.

The neon lights and pulsing music offered temporary refuge. But the cost—financially, emotionally, and spiritually—was steep.

It wasn't about the clubs themselves. It was about the void I was trying to fill. I was a man who had spent nearly two decades providing, protecting, and believing. And suddenly, I was alone. The addiction didn't start with desire; it started with despair.

But somewhere in the haze, something unexpected happened.

Not every night was a blur of numbness. Somewhere between the sets and the shadows, I met a couple of women who saw past the performance. They weren't just dancers—they were people. Women with dreams, children, heartbreaks, and stories that mirrored my own in ways I never expected.

One of them—let's call her Tasha—had a laugh that could cut through the noise. She was sharp, funny, and unapologetically real. We talked between sets—not about fantasy, but about life. She told me about her son, her side hustle selling handmade jewelry, and her dream of opening a boutique. I told her about my divorce, my loneliness, and my confusion. And she listened. Really listened.

Another—Renee—was quieter. Thoughtful. She'd sit with me when the club was slow, sipping water and asking questions no one else bothered to ask. "What do you miss most about your old life?" she asked once. I didn't know how to answer. But the question stayed with me.

These women didn't try to fix me. They didn't pretend to be anything they weren't. But in their presence, I felt something I hadn't felt in a long time: human. Seen. Not judged.

I stopped going as often—not because I was cured, but because I no longer needed the illusion. The friendships I formed with Tasha and Renee reminded me that healing doesn't always come from the expected places. Sometimes it shows up in the middle of a storm, wearing glitter and heels, offering you a seat and a moment of truth.

The Turning Point

It wasn't a single moment that changed me; it was the slow unraveling of the lies I'd been telling myself. I wasn't just lonely—I was grieving. Grieving the loss of a life I had built, the identity I had wrapped around being a husband, a provider, a protector.

And in the middle of that grief, I found two people—Tasha and Renee—who didn't try to fix me, seduce me, or sell me anything. They just showed up.

Tasha once said, "You don't have to pretend here. We all wear masks, but you can take yours off with me."

At the time, I was still struggling with the guilt and fear of having left the church—wondering if I had abandoned God's people and unsure of what my spiritual future would look like. Then Renee said something that pierced deeper than any sermon I'd heard: "Some people are only meant to be in your life for a season. Sometimes we make the mistake of trying to make temporary people permanent."

That hit me harder than any lap dance ever could. There I was, sitting in a strip club, being taught wisdom by a 23-year-old stripper. Yet, it was the first time I felt safe enough to be vulnerable again.

Renee was the one who challenged me most. "You keep coming here like you're looking for something," she said. "But maybe what you're looking for isn't in this room. Maybe it's in you."

I didn't know whether to be offended or grateful. Turns out, I was both.

Their words stayed with me. Their friendship gave me something I hadn't felt in months—dignity. Not because they treated me like a man with money, but because they treated me like a man with a story. And slowly, I started to believe I was worth more than the shame I carried.

The Beginning of Healing

I began to pull back—not out of guilt, but out of clarity. I didn't need the clubs anymore. I needed truth. I needed connection. I needed to rebuild.

I started journaling. I went to therapy. I reconnected with old friends. And I kept in touch with Tasha and Renee—not as distractions, but as reminders that healing can come from the most unexpected places.

They were part of my story—not the scandalous part, but the sacred part. The part where grace showed up in glitter and eyeliner and reminded me that even in the darkest places, light finds a way in.

Healing didn't come to me in a church pew or a therapist's office—not at first. It came in dimly lit rooms where people wore masks, but a few dared to take them off. It came through conversations with women who had every reason to be guarded, yet chose to be kind. It came through laughter, honesty, and the quiet realization that I wasn't alone.

Tasha and Renee didn't save me. But they reminded me that I was worth saving. They reminded me that connection is possible, even when you feel unworthy of it. And they reminded me that grace doesn't always wear white robes—it sometimes shows up in stilettos and eyeliner, offering you a moment of truth when you least expect it.

I'm still on the journey. Still healing. Still learning to forgive myself. But I carry those friendships with me like lanterns in the dark—proof that even in the places we're taught to avoid, God can still speak.

As time went on, the pull of old habits crept back in. I was spending so much money feeding my strip club addiction that a voice inside me began to whisper, You need to stop wasting money on this and put it toward something that might give you more in return. That was the moment I picked up a new habit—gambling. I had traded one addiction for another.

Trading Shadows: When One Addiction Replaces Another

I thought I was making a smarter choice. Strip clubs drained my wallet and left me feeling emptier each time. So when that voice whispered, At least with gambling, you might win something, it felt like logic. It felt like progress.

But addiction doesn't care what form it takes—it just wants to keep you chasing.

I didn't realize I was swapping one illusion for another. The flashing lights of the casino, the thrill of the bet, the hope that this time I'd hit big—it was all just another mask. Another way to numb the ache. Another way to avoid the silence that asked me to face myself.

And yet, even in that spiral, God didn't stop speaking. Not in thunder or fire, but in quiet moments. In the regret after a loss. In the kindness of a stranger who saw through my bravado. In the friendships I carried like lanterns—reminders that I was still worthy of light.

I'm not proud of the choices I made. But I'm proud that I can name them now. That I can look at my story without flinching. That I can say: I'm still healing. Still learning. Still walking toward grace.

The Mirage of Winning

At first, gambling felt like a solution. Strip clubs had drained me emotionally and financially, but gambling whispered promises of redemption. You could win it all back, it said. You could fix everything. And I believed it.

I started small—scratch-offs, a few rounds of blackjack, some late-night poker games. But soon, I was chasing the rush. The thrill of risk. The illusion of control. I convinced myself I was being strategic, that this was a smarter addiction.

But the truth? I was still running. Still trying to fill the same void with a different poison.

There were nights I won big, and those wins were dangerous. They made me believe I was onto something —that I could outsmart the system, that I could gamble my way out of the pain.

But the losses always came. And when they did, they hit harder than any lap dance ever could.

The Dashboard – When the Voice Finally Broke Through

It was late—the kind of late where the world feels quiet enough for your thoughts to echo. I was parked outside the casino, the neon glow still flickering in my rearview mirror. I had lost more than I could afford. Again.

But this time, it wasn't just the money. It was me. I felt sick—not just in my stomach, but in my soul.

I stared at the dashboard like it held the answers. Like maybe if I looked long enough, it would light up with a message from God, or wisdom, or even just a reason.

And then the voice came.

Not the one that had led me into gambling. Not the one that whispered promises of escape and adrenaline. But the one that had always been there—quiet, steady, patient.

This isn't who you are.

It was the same message Tasha and Renee had told me back at the strip clubs. The same truth I had tried to drown in distraction. The same whisper I had ignored for too long.

I didn't argue. I didn't bargain. I just cried.

Because I knew it was right.

I had spent years trying to outrun pain—through religion, through rebellion, through addiction. But pain doesn't get outrun. It gets faced.

And that night, in the silence of my car, I finally stopped running.

I didn't have a plan. I didn't have a solution. But I had a moment of truth.

And sometimes, that's where healing begins.

Fear Times Ten – When Addiction Reveals the Void

I had never felt fear like the fear I felt while gambling.

Not the fear of losing a hand or watching chips disappear—but the fear of losing myself. The fear of knowing I couldn't survive if I kept going, but also knowing I couldn't stop.

It started with fear. Fear of not having enough. Fear of being left behind. Fear of the silence that came after the chaos.

Gambling offered a temporary fix—a rush, a distraction—but it didn't cure the fear. It multiplied it. What began as a way to cope became a trap. The same fear that led me to the casino now followed me out of it—times ten.

And then it hit me.

Addiction isn't just about desire—it's about despair. It's about trying to fill a void that only faith can fill.

I realized my addiction was a symptom of something deeper: a lack of trust. A lack of belief that God would provide, that healing was possible, that I was still worthy of peace.

I had spent years believing in a distorted version of faith—one built on fear, control, and punishment. But real faith? Real faith is surrender. Real faith is trust. Real faith is knowing that even when you have nothing, you're still held.

That night, sitting in my car outside the casino, I felt the weight of it all—the money lost, the time wasted, the slow unraveling of my soul.

And I heard the voice again: This isn't who you are.

I didn't argue. I didn't run. I just cried.

Because I knew it was true.

The Shift Toward Healing

Healing didn't come overnight. It came in small decisions—in choosing not to walk into the casino, in calling a friend instead, in praying when I felt the urge to escape. In remembering the words of Tasha and Renee, who saw me not as a broken man, but as a man in process.

I started to see addiction not as a failure, but as a signal—an alarm that something deeper needed attention. I wasn't just addicted to gambling or strip clubs. I was addicted to avoiding pain, to numbing grief, to silencing the questions I didn't want to answer.

But now, I'm answering them. One by one.

Closing Reflection: The Long Road Back

I'm still on the journey—still healing, still learning to forgive myself. But I've stopped chasing illusions. I've stopped trading one shadow for another. And I've started walking toward the light—slowly, deliberately, with grace.

Because even in the darkest places, God still speaks. And sometimes, the most powerful victories begin with surrender.

CHAPTER 13
THE BANANA AND THE BIBLE STUDY

A Safe Place to Speak

After leaving the House of Prayer, I moved in with my cousin—someone who had also escaped the grip of the cult. Living with her felt like stepping into sunlight after years in the dark. We talked for hours, sharing memories, unpacking trauma, and slowly rebuilding trust in ourselves and each other. She became my best friend, my confidant, and my anchor.

One evening, as we sat talking in her living room, there was a knock at the door. It was another former member of the House of Prayer—someone who had left when she was just a girl. I hadn't seen her in years, and her visit felt like a reunion of survivors. We welcomed her in, sat down, and began catching up.

Then she asked a question that changed the entire tone of the evening.

"Did you hear about the banana?"

I frowned. "No... what about a banana?"

She looked at my cousin, then back at me. "Your cousin didn't tell you?"

"No," I said slowly. "What happened?"

Her voice dropped. "The 'Man of God' tried to use a banana on your sister."

I froze. "What?"

She explained that one night, the cult leader—who was also my sister's husband—had attempted to initiate intimacy but was unable to perform. In a moment of twisted desperation, he reached for a banana and tried to use it as a substitute. My sister was horrified. She shouted, resisted, and demanded to know what he was doing.

He dismissed her outrage, told her she was overreacting, and claimed there was nothing wrong with his actions. But my sister knew better. She told him she was going to bring the matter before the church.

That might sound strange to outsiders, but in the House of Prayer, domestic issues were often handled publicly—especially when the "Man of God" wasn't the one being accused. But this time was different. His own wife was calling him out. And, ironically, there was a Bible study scheduled that very night.

The Culture of Control

This wasn't just about a banana. It was about power. About humiliation. About a man who believed he was above accountability—even in the most intimate parts of marriage. And it was about a system that enabled him, protected him, and silenced those who dared to speak out.

Hearing this story shook me. Not just because of what happened to my sister, but because I had once believed in this man. I had once defended him. I had once helped build the very system that allowed this kind of abuse to thrive.

But now, I was listening. I was learning. And I was preparing to speak.

CHAPTER 14
THE THEATER OF SHAME

A Rigged Trial in Sacred Clothing

That night at Bible study, the "Man of God" arrived with his wife—my sister—and immediately took control of the room. Before anyone could speak, before my sister could share her truth, he made a calculated move: he ordered all the children to be removed from the sanctuary. The usher obeyed, sending them into the parking lot —shielding them from what was about to unfold, or perhaps shielding himself from their innocent eyes.

He stood before the congregation and announced that he and his wife had a "problem" to bring before the church. But it wasn't a confession—it was a performance. He wanted to get ahead of the story, to control the narrative before my sister could open her mouth.

He said, "I was engaging in sexual activity with my wife, but could not perform. In the heat of the moment, I grabbed an object from the nightstand and tried to insert it into her. She rejected me and said I disrespected her."

He never named the object. He never acknowledged the violation. And he never gave my sister a chance to speak.

Instead, he turned to the congregation and asked for their opinion. One by one, the leaders spoke—not in defense of my sister, but in condemnation. They said she was overreacting. That she was wrong. That she had disrespected the "Man of God."

Then he turned to my mother.

She looked at my sister and said, "You were wrong to call him out. You need to learn to keep your mouth shut."

The rebukes came like waves. My sister sat there, surrounded by people who claimed to love her, being publicly shamed for resisting an act of sexual violation. Eventually, she raised her hand. Submitted. Apologized. Not because she believed she was wrong, but because she knew justice would never come in his house, under his rules, in his kingdom.

A Double Standard Etched in Stone

And I couldn't help but think: what if it had been me?

If I had done what he did—if I had tried to use a banana on my wife—I would have been dragged through the coals. The children wouldn't have been sent out. They would have been brought in. Made to witness. Made to rebuke. Made to remember.

I would have been made a public disgrace. Not just for a night—for years.

But him? He walked away untouched. His power intact. His image preserved.

The Cost of Silence

This wasn't just a moment of injustice. It was a ritual of control. A demonstration of how deeply the cult had been conditioned to protect its leader at all costs—even at the expense of truth, dignity, and basic human decency.

My sister's voice was stolen that night. But her story lives. And now, so does mine.

CHAPTER 15
THE BANANA MAN AND THE FALL OF THE ILLUSION

The Crime of Wounding Pride

When I learned about the banana incident, I knew my sister's days of being protected—or even tolerated—were over. In the House of Prayer, the worst crime a woman could commit wasn't adultery, rebellion, or even blasphemy. It was wounding the pride of the "Man of God."

For years, he had boasted about his sexual prowess. Despite being nearly seventy, he claimed he could satisfy a young wife with ease. It was part of his myth—proof that he was still virile, still powerful, still chosen. My sister, barely thirty when they married, was supposed to be the living evidence of that claim.

But now, because of her, the truth had slipped out: he couldn't perform. And worse, he had tried to use a banana as a substitute. That revelation didn't just embarrass him—it shattered the image he had spent decades building.

And when the "Man of God's" ego is bruised, someone always pays.

My sister became the target. Not because she spoke out, but because she existed as a reminder of his failure. Her silence wasn't enough. Her apology wasn't enough. He needed someone to blame for the whispers, the mockery, the cracks forming in his authority.

Then came the moment that sealed her fate.

During an argument with my soon-to-be ex-wife, I mentioned the banana incident. I called him "The Banana Man." It was a moment of anger, of truth, of rebellion. And she—perhaps out of spite, perhaps out of loyalty—told him.

Now he knew that I knew. That I was laughing. That I was armed with the one thing he couldn't defend against: the truth.

And he blamed my sister.

In his mind, she had betrayed him twice. First, by rejecting his act. Then by allowing the story to spread. I became his enemy, but she became the reason I had ammunition. And in a system built on control, that made her dangerous.

The Cult of Ego

This wasn't just about a banana. It was about power. About image. About a man who believed he was above reproach, and a congregation conditioned to protect that illusion at all costs.

My sister didn't just hurt his pride—she exposed his humanity. And in the House of Prayer, that was unforgivable.

CHAPTER 16
UNDIVIDED ATTENTION

The Hour of Control

It was sometime after the banana incident—after the illusion of the "Man of God's" invincibility had begun to crack—that another act of violence unfolded. The congregation was deep into one of his infamous marathon services, stretching into the early hours of the morning. Around 3:00 a.m., my sister, exhausted, began to drift off. I spoke of this incident in earlier chapters.

That's when he snapped.

"You'd better wake up before I have these men drag your ass to the back," he barked across the sanctuary. It wasn't a metaphor. It was a threat, and everyone knew it. In the House of Prayer, "the back" was where punishments happened. It was where men, handpicked for loyalty, enforced discipline with their belts and switches.

My sister, startled and humiliated, tried to defuse the moment. “I’m sorry, sweetheart. I’ll try not to fall asleep again.”

But it wasn’t enough.

She pulled out her phone—maybe to stay awake, maybe just to mentally escape. He saw it. And in an instant, he was on her. He snatched the phone from her hand, slammed it onto the concrete floor, and stomped it into shards.

“Don’t be looking at no phone while I’m talking!” he roared. “Give me your undivided attention!”

The room fell silent. No one moved. No one breathed. The message was clear: no one— not even his wife—was safe from his wrath.

The Reprogramming Begins

From that night on, he began to turn the congregation against her. At first, it was subtle—comments about loyalty, about obedience, about how a wife should reflect her husband’s authority. Then, the remarks grew sharper, public, and cruel.

“Maybe I married the wrong woman,” he’d say. “She won’t let me lead her.”

He didn’t need to say more. The congregation,

trained to mirror his moods and echo his judgments, followed his lead. They began to treat her with coldness, disrespect, and silent condemnation. Her status as "First Lady" no longer meant anything. She had failed the only test that mattered in his world: absolute submission.

The Legacy of Abuse

Even now, long after that night, the mistreatment continues. The congregation still follows the programming. They still see her not as a victim, but as a traitor. Not as someone who endured humiliation, threats, and violence, but as someone who dared to challenge the "Man of God."

And that's the cruelest part of all. In a system like this, truth becomes rebellion. Dignity becomes defiance. And survival becomes a sin.

CHAPTER 17
THE TAPE AND THE TRUTH

A Father's Dream on the Brink

All my life, I wanted to be a family man—not just a provider, but a protector. A father who showed up. A father who stayed. I dreamed of raising sons who knew they were loved and daughters who knew they were safe. And by the grace of God, I had twelve children—five sons and seven daughters. I had everything I ever prayed for.

And I was on the verge of losing it all.

The Retaliation Begins

When I learned what the "Man of God" had done to my sister—his own wife—I knew retaliation was coming. I had crossed a line. I had seen behind the curtain. And in a system built on secrecy and control, truth is the greatest threat.

I didn't know how he would strike, but I knew it would be personal.

So the day I went to pick up my children, I came prepared. I wore a tape recorder. I needed proof—not just for myself, but for the court. For the truth.

The Scene That Broke Me

What I captured on that tape was the most degrading moment of my life.

My wife—on all fours—barking like a dog. My children, encouraged by her, shouting insults at me. Calling me names no child should ever say to their father. Words that didn't come from their hearts, but from someone else's script.

It wasn't just disrespect—it was indoctrination. It was a performance designed to humiliate me, to provoke me, to alienate my children's love from me.

And it worked. Not because I believed their words, but because I saw the pain behind them. I saw my children being used as weapons in a war they didn't understand.

The Fight for Justice

I filed a complaint. I submitted the tape. I stood before the court not as a perfect man, but as a father fighting for his children. I wanted the judge to hear it all—to understand the depth of manipulation, to see the fingerprints of the "Man of God" all over this act of cruelty.

This wasn't just about visitation. It was about restoration. About reclaiming the love that had been stolen. About proving that no amount of spiritual abuse could erase the truth of who I was: their father.

CHAPTER 18
THE COURTROOM CONFESSION

The Surprise

When I arrived at the hearing, I was hit with a surprise. My wife had a new attorney. Her first lawyer—a young white woman appointed by Legal Aid—had quietly withdrawn from the case. No explanation. Just gone.

I had my suspicions why. Maybe she saw too much. Maybe she sensed what was coming.

Her replacement was an older Black woman—seasoned, confident, and privately retained. Because of a prior ruling, I was responsible for paying her fees. I couldn't afford my own representation, but I had to pay for hers. Still, I didn't flinch. My focus wasn't on money. It was on saving my children.

The Tape That Didn't Matter

The judge opened the hearing by acknowledging the contempt charge I had filed. She asked me to explain. I told her everything—how I arrived for court-ordered visitation, how my wife was on all fours barking like a dog, how she called me vile names, and worst of all, how she encouraged our children to do the same.

I told the judge I had recorded the incident. I had the tape. I was ready to let the truth speak for itself.

But her attorney objected.

"He didn't have my client's permission to record her," she said.

The judge sustained the objection. The tape was inadmissible.

I was crushed. I had hoped the tape would expose the cruelty of what I was up against. But then, something unexpected happened.

The Confession

The judge turned to my wife. "Mrs. Oglesby, is it true that you had your children call their father those disgusting and disrespectful names?"

Without hesitation, my wife said, "I sure did! I told them to call him those names because it's the truth!"

Her attorney panicked. "Objection, Your Honor! May I consult with my client?"

The judge allowed it. But everyone in the courtroom heard what had just been said.

Her lawyer leaned in and whispered, "Mrs. Oglesby, you need to say you were upset and that you're sorry."

My wife looked her lawyer in the eye and said, "I'm not apologizing. I'm not sorry."

The judge was stunned. She tried to reason with her. "Divorce is emotional. People lash out. But involving the children crosses a line. Do you agree?"

"No," my wife said. "I do not agree."

It was like watching someone in self-destruct mode, programmed by the "Man of God" to sabotage herself without even realizing it.

The Judgment

The judge found her in contempt of court. Then she turned to me.

"Mr. Oglesby, what do you want me to do?"

I paused. I didn't want vengeance. I didn't want my children's mother in jail. I wanted peace. I wanted healing. I wanted my children to have both parents, even if one was lost in a fog of manipulation.

I asked the judge to issue a stern warning—to

explain the consequences, to give her a chance to change.

Because I knew how the "Man of God" operated. If she were arrested, he'd turn it into a media circus. He'd spin the story into a lie: a mother of twelve jailed for protecting her children. He'd call the press. He'd weaponize the moment. And the truth would be buried under headlines.

The judge agreed. She showed wisdom. She saw the trap, and she sidestepped it.

The Aftermath

I hoped the warning would be enough. I hoped my wife would see the danger of her path. But deep down, I knew she wasn't acting alone. The "Man of God" wasn't finished.

And neither was I.

CHAPTER 19
VISITATION DENIED

THE WAR FOR MY CHILDREN'S HEARTS

The Setup

On July 23, 2012, I arrived at my children's home for a scheduled visitation. After the contempt of court hearing, I expected things to go smoother. I had the legal right to see my kids. I had hope.

But hope doesn't always hold up against manipulation.

My wife opened the door with hostility. "What do you want?" she asked.

"I'm here to pick up the kids for my weekend visitation," I replied. "Where are they?"

Her answer was chilling. "I can't let you get the kids because I don't know where they are."

I stared at her. "How can you not know where your twelve children are? Did you lose them somewhere?"

She repeated, "They're not here. I don't know what happened to them."

I knew she was playing games. And I knew exactly who was behind it—the so-called Man of God who had orchestrated so much of our pain.

The Police Report

I went straight to the police station and explained the situation. An officer agreed to follow me back to the house. This time, my wife didn't answer the door. My seventeen-year-old son did.

The officer asked, "Where are your mother and your brothers and sisters?"

"They're not here," he said. "I don't know where they are."

Then the officer asked, "Are you going with your dad? It's his weekend to have visitation."

My son looked at me and said, "No. He abandoned us."

I was stunned. "How can you say I abandoned you when your mother had me put out of the house and filed for divorce?"

His response cut deep. "When you left the church,

you left us. If you don't want the church, then we don't want you."

The officer later wrote in his report that my son had a "possessed" look on his face when he said it. That wasn't my son speaking. That was indoctrination. That was poison planted by people who wanted to sever our bond permanently.

The Next Day

I returned the next day, still determined to see my children. My wife opened the door again.

"What do you want?" she asked.

"I'm here to pick up the kids," I said.

Her response was filled with venom and hate. She refused to let them go. She made it clear that she would not honor the court order, and she would not honor my role as their father.

This was more than defiance. It was spiritual warfare disguised as parental conflict. They were trying to break me. They wanted me to give up.

But giving up was never an option.

They didn't understand how deeply I loved my children. They didn't understand that I wasn't just fighting for visitation—I was fighting for their freedom. For their minds. For their souls.

And I would keep fighting. No matter how long it took.

I returned the next day, still determined to see my children. My wife opened the door again.

"What do you want?" she asked.

"I'm here to pick up the kids," I said.

Her response was filled with venom. She refused to honor the court order. She refused to acknowledge my role as their father. Her words came sharp and cruel—racial slurs, personal attacks, and a complete disregard for the law.

She sneered, "I don't care what the judge said, and I don't care if you file another contempt of court charge. I'm not turning my kids over to you! So, get out of my yard! I wish I'd never let you touch me!"

And just for irony's sake, she said it all while wearing her long, floor-length church dress—modest on the outside, but her words anything but holy.

I reminded her of the consequences. "You can go to jail for disobeying a judge's order. If you don't send my children out here right now, I'll file another contempt of court charge against you."

She didn't flinch. "I don't care what the judge said. My kids are not going anywhere with you."

Her tone was vicious, her words cutting. But I stood firm—because I knew what was at stake.

The Bigger Battle

This wasn't just about visitation. It was about control. It was about a toxic ideology that had taken root in my family and turned love into leverage.

They wanted me to give up. They wanted me to walk away. But they underestimated the depth of my love.

They didn't understand that I wasn't just fighting for weekends—I was fighting for my children's minds, their hearts, their freedom. I was fighting against a system that used religion as a weapon and turned my children into pawns.

But I would not be broken. I would not be silenced. And I would never stop fighting for my children.

CHAPTER 20
THE COURTHOUSE TRAP

A Father's Determination

After yet another weekend of denied visitation, I walked into the courthouse with a heavy heart but a clear purpose. I had filed a second contempt of court charge against my wife for violating the judge's order. I wasn't just fighting for time; I was fighting for my children's right to know their father.

As I approached the courtroom, a voice rang out—bright, innocent, and full of love.

"Hey, Daddy!" my youngest son Philip shouted. "Look, everybody, there go my daddy!"

For a moment, the world stopped. That single cry pierced through months of silence and rejection. But before I could respond, a voice from the crowd snapped back, "Sit down, boy! Don't be acting like you happy to see him!"

It was a member of the Man of God's congregation. Their control over my children was so complete that even joy had become forbidden.

The Setup

To my surprise, nearly all of my children were there—except my two oldest sons. I greeted them with warmth, holding onto that small moment of connection before stepping into the courtroom. But as I crossed the threshold, it hit me: this wasn't a coincidence. It was a setup.

The Man of God had orchestrated their presence. He anticipated that the judge might hold my wife accountable, possibly even jail her for contempt. So he staged a scene: twelve children in the courtroom, ready to cry and plead for their mother. Cameras would roll. Emotions would flare. And the media would have its story: a mother of twelve, dragged away in front of her children.

It was a tactic he'd mastered. Years earlier, when DFCS intervened in his cult and removed forty-nine children to protect them from ritualistic abuse, he turned the tables. He coached the children to resist. He made sure the media were there. He weaponized emotion and optics to paint himself as the victim and the authorities as the villains.

But this time was different.

He may have fooled DFCS. He may have manipulated the public. But he wasn't going to fool me.

I knew my enemy. I knew his playbook. And I knew that behind the tears and the spectacle was a strategy designed to destroy me.

CHAPTER 21
THE WISDOM OF THE COURT

The Setup

I knew my enemy. I knew his playbook. Behind the tears and the spectacle was a calculated attempt to silence me, to shame me, and to sever my bond with my children. But I wasn't there for a show. I was there for justice.

When the judge called our case, I stood and stated my reason clearly: my wife had refused, for the second time, to honor the court's visitation order. I had filed a contempt of court charge—not out of spite, but out of necessity. My children deserved to know their father, and I deserved the right to be in their lives.

The judge listened and then suggested mediation. She made it clear: if we couldn't reach an agreement, my wife would be held in contempt and face jail time. But I could tell—she didn't want to lock my wife up. And I couldn't help but wonder: if the roles were reversed, would the court show me the same restraint?

The Mediation

In private chambers, we sat with the mediator—my wife, her attorney, and me. For thirty minutes, we went back and forth. Her reasoning was vague, evasive. The only clear objection she had was that I was no longer a member of the "Man of God's" congregation.

Her attorney urged her to comply, warning that continued defiance would not only land her in jail but could cost her the case entirely. Still, she didn't budge.

Then the mediator turned to me. "Why do you think your wife is being so defiant?"

I paused, then asked, "Are you and the judge aware that my wife brought ten of our children to court today?"

The mediator looked surprised. "No, we weren't aware. Are they really here?"

"Yes," I said. "They're in the visitors' lobby. And the reason she's being so defiant is because she wants the judge to lock her up. She wants the children to witness it, to cry, to plead. She wants a scene. Because the 'Man of God' is planning to use it for the media: to paint her as a victim and me as the villain."

The mediator's expression shifted. Without another

word, she ended the session and sent us back to the courtroom.

The Judge's Wisdom

Back in court, the judge was waiting. "I've been informed that no agreement could be reached," she said. "I've also been informed that the children are here today. Is this true, Mrs. Oglesby?"

"Yes," my wife replied. "All of my minor children are here."

"How many?" the judge asked.

"Ten."

The judge didn't flinch. "I want the deputies to retrieve all of the children and take them to a separate part of the courthouse."

Then she turned to me. "Mr. Oglesby, do you have transportation?"

"Yes," I said. "I can call my cousin. She has a van."

"Good," the judge said. "Call her. I'm ordering the children to be turned over to you today. You will have them for four days to make up for the visitation time you were denied."

She then addressed my wife. "You are found in contempt of court again. This will not reflect well at your final divorce and custody hearing."

Finally, she turned back to me. "Mr. Oglesby, go to

the chambers where your children are. No one else will be allowed to accompany you. You will be escorted out by deputies until you and your children leave the premises."

The Victory Behind the Curtain

I could tell by the judge's tone and precision that the mediator had informed her of the plan. The judge saw through the spectacle. She used wisdom to dismantle the trap before it could be sprung.

The "Man of God" had underestimated her and me.

That day, I didn't just walk out of the courthouse with my children. I walked out with proof that truth, when spoken boldly and backed by love, can outmaneuver even the most calculated deception.

I wasn't there for a show. I was there for justice.

CHAPTER 22
THE BREAKING POINT

The Walk of Tension

As I escorted my children out of the courthouse, their voices rang out in confusion and resistance.

"Where are we going?"

"We don't want to go with you!"

Their words stung, but their feet kept moving. They followed my instructions, stayed close, and didn't resist physically. I watched their body language—tense but compliant. I knew what I was seeing: loyalty torn between truth and indoctrination.

They were still under the influence of the "Man of God." And I understood. I had once been under his spell, too. I had welcomed him into our lives, believing he was a force for good. I had helped build the very prison I was now trying to free my children from.

The Sheraton Weekend

I wanted to give them joy. I wanted to remind them of who I was—not the villain painted by others, but their father. So I booked a two-bedroom suite at the Sheraton, right across from Cumberland Mall. Pools, comfort, laughter—I hoped it would be a weekend of healing.

The younger kids lit up with excitement. The pool was their world for those few days. But my older daughters were distant, withdrawn. I gave them space, hoping time would soften the edges. Still, something felt off. They kept slipping away, and when they returned, their energy was colder.

Later, one of the younger children quietly revealed the truth: their mother had given my oldest daughter a phone. They were speaking to the "Man of God" in secret. He was feeding them lines, coaching them on how to confront me.

The Confrontation

Back at the hotel, my oldest daughter approached me.

"Daddy, can we talk?"

I welcomed the moment, hoping for connection, for a chance to bridge the distance. But instead, I was met with words that weren't hers—words that were weaponized, vulgar, and meant to provoke.

I tried to respond calmly. I explained my intentions, my love, my hope. But then came the final blow—words so cruel and degrading that something inside me snapped. I flipped the glass coffee table. It shattered across the floor.

In that moment, I felt something I had never allowed myself to feel before: hate.

Not toward my children. Not even toward my wife. But toward the "Man of God." He had orchestrated this. He had poisoned the well. And I had played right into his hands.

The Fallout

I knew I had messed up. I called Janet, hoping for comfort, but she gave me truth instead.

"There's no judge alive who will give custody to a man who can't control his temper."

Her words cut deep, but they were honest.

I needed guidance. I reached out to someone I respected deeply—a former Head Judge of Fulton County Superior Court. She welcomed me into her home. I told her everything, tears streaming down my face. I didn't hold back.

And she gave me something I hadn't expected: hope.

"Michael," she said, "tell the judge exactly what you told me. Don't mince words. Judges don't just look at what you did—they want to understand why. They want the story. And your story matters."

The Turning Point

That conversation didn't erase the damage, but it gave me a path forward. It reminded me that redemption isn't found in perfection—it's found in honesty, humility, and the courage to keep showing up.

During one of the most difficult seasons of my life, my wife filed abandonment charges against me, and I was summoned to court. I wasn't worried about the charge itself; there were no grounds for it. I hadn't abandoned my family. I had been put out of the house, yet I continued to pay all the bills.

What puzzled me most was why a "Man of God" would advise her to file such a claim. Even more confusing was the fact that she came to court without an attorney.

I felt confident I would beat the charge, but what truly haunted me was the incident at the hotel where I lost my temper and shattered a glass table near my children. I feared that this moment would be brought up in court.

I was prepared to follow the advice of a judge friend: be honest, tell the full story, and hold nothing back. But to my surprise, my wife never mentioned the hotel incident to the judge. I knew she knew about it—she told me herself after one of my long visits with the kids. She even said she planned to bring it up at the next hearing. Why she chose not to, I still don't understand. But I thank God for covering me.

That's why songs like *Marvin Sapp's Never Would Have Made It* bring me to tears. I truly believe I would have lost everything, but now I see how God was with me all along. His favor was evident.

Not long after that hearing, I received a letter from the court stating that my wife's second attorney had withdrawn from representing her. No reason was given, but based on her lack of cooperation in front of the judge, I had a good idea why. The attorney even called me personally to say she wouldn't require me to pay her fees, despite the court's order. That spoke volumes.

Two attorneys had now walked away from representing my wife, and the judge had witnessed her defiance firsthand. It was clear the tide was turning. Everything seemed to be shifting in my favor—and what came next was even more remarkable.

My Son's Awakening

It had been a year since the divorce was filed, and my life felt hollow without my family. I cried every day and every night, gripped by the fear of losing them.

One afternoon, while riding with a friend, I felt a deep disturbance in my spirit. My friend noticed something was wrong and pulled the car over to check on me. I told her, "I feel my son's spirit in mine—as if he's in trouble." It's hard to explain, but I knew something wasn't right with my oldest son.

She tried to comfort me, but the feeling lingered. I knew that whenever I interacted with my wife and children, my wife would lead them in a campaign of disrespect and demonization against me. But my oldest son never joined in. That took courage—because in the House of Prayer cult, anyone who refused to vilify me, the so-called "Public Enemy #1," was seen as an enemy of God himself. I knew my son would face verbal and, possibly, physical abuse for standing firm.

The next day, I received a call from a young woman —my children's cousin on their mother's side—who had once been part of the cult but had left years earlier. She had been close to our family and often babysat our kids. She told me my son was staying at her house. His mother had thrown him out, following the "Man of God's" instruction, because he refused to disrespect me.

I asked her to have him call me, but she said he wasn't ready. I understood. After years of hearing poisonous rhetoric, it takes time to trust—especially someone who has been the target of that hate. She promised to care for him and keep me informed.

That moment—my son being cast out—was the beginning of the unraveling. My children are close, and they love their older brother deeply. His absence shook them. They were already conflicted about me not being in the home, and now this added another layer of pain. My son's influence on his siblings was strong, and I saw this development as a turning point.

I began to understand why my spirit had been so troubled. The Bible speaks of "the troubling of the waters"—how once a year, God would stir the waters, and whoever stepped in with faith would be healed. God was troubling the waters in my life because He was preparing to bless me. But I knew there would be suffering and tribulation before the blessing came.

I had always prepared my son to be self-sufficient. I taught him to work hard and never accepted the cult's belief that children only needed the "three R's"—Reading, 'Riting, and 'Rithmetic—and no education beyond sixth grade. Even under the cult's influence, I wanted more for my children. When my son reached the limits of their so-called homeschooling program, I found an outside program to help him earn his GED.

He later attended trade school and became an electrician.

The Bible says, "Work with your own hands, that ye may lack nothing." I raised all twelve of my children with this principle. My goal was for them to be self-sufficient, able to thrive without depending on anyone. If a parent fails to instill that, they've failed their children.

The "Man of God" thrives on dependency. He gives members cash, homes, cars—not out of generosity, but to keep them indebted and under control. That's not God's way. God wants us to lack nothing and to walk in freedom, not bondage.

I've seen many people leave the cult only to end up in poverty, abusive relationships, or jail. Not because they were cursed, but because they were never taught how to survive. It's a setup. The "Man of God" tells them they'll fall without him—and it seems true, because he's made sure they're unprepared. But when you invest in yourself and your children, you break that cycle. You escape.

With signs pointing toward me gaining custody, I began preparing. I found a three-bedroom apartment and furnished it with love and care. I decorated the girls' room with pretty curtains and matching bedding, and gave the boys a space of their own.

Soon after, I received a call from the court-appointed

Guardian ad Litem. She wanted to meet me at my new home.

When she arrived, she asked, "Why do you feel you should have custody of your children?"

I answered, "Because at least fifteen to twenty children were molested by a member of the 'Man of God's' congregation—and instead of reporting him, they're harboring him. Three of those children were mine. I turned him in, and he's now serving a ten-year sentence. But my wife and the 'Man of God' disagreed with me for doing the right thing."

I also told her I had met with the head of the homeschooling program in Atlanta and discovered that all the children in the House of Prayer were registered as 'special needs'—including mine. There was no medical evidence to support this. It was a loophole to avoid state testing and hide the fact that these children weren't being properly educated.

I wanted my children placed in public schools where they could learn, grow, and be free.

I also shared with the Guardian ad Litem the disturbing practices within the "Man of God's" organization: how young girls, some as young as fourteen, were forced into arranged marriages with grown men and pressured to bear as many children as possible. I told her plainly that I did not want this to be the only future available to my daughters. I refused to let them be trapped in a system that stripped them of choice, dignity, and opportunity.

I also expressed my deep concern about the cult's belief in ritualistic beatings of children, where multiple men would physically discipline them under the guise of spiritual correction. I could not allow my children to be subjected to that kind of abuse.

The Guardian ad Litem listened carefully and told me she planned to have the children tested by the state to determine their actual academic levels. Then she asked, "Is there anyone else I can speak to who can corroborate what you're saying?"

That's when it struck me—I needed to tell her about my oldest son. I explained that he was no longer part of the cult and had firsthand experience with the abuse and manipulation. I suggested she speak with him directly.

She agreed. She said she would meet with my son and share the outcome of that conversation with the judge at our final divorce hearing.

After nearly two years of turmoil, the final court date for our divorce hearing had arrived. Just a week before, I received an unexpected phone call from an attorney in Atlanta. She told me that a colleague had shared my story with her, and she felt compelled to offer her services. She was an intelligent African American woman, well-versed in the workings of the Fulton County courthouse.

After hearing the details of my case, she said, "You don't need much—just someone with legal experience to present this properly to the judge. And while it's rare for a judge to remove ten children from their mother and award custody to the father, your circumstances are unique. I believe you have a strong chance."

When I asked about her fee, she said, "I'll only charge you $500." I was stunned. This was the kind of attorney I had prayed for, someone who believed in my cause and saw the truth. I would've paid far more, but she asked for so little. I accepted immediately.

When we arrived at the courthouse, my wife was there without legal representation. She announced to the judge that she would be representing herself. Then came the surprise: she declared that she no longer wanted a divorce and was withdrawing her petition.

The judge looked puzzled. "After nearly two years, why are you withdrawing now?"

My wife replied, "The Bible says the only legitimate reason for divorce is adultery or fornication, and my husband hasn't committed adultery."

She spoke as if she and the "Man of God" had just discovered this scripture, but I knew better. He was the one who taught me that verse years ago. The truth was, they realized the case wasn't going their way. This was a last-minute attempt to regain control.

It was then I realized that the six thousand dollars I had paid my first attorney—money I once regretted spending—was worth every penny. When I first met him, he asked me, "Do you really want this divorce to go through?" He explained that he had seen cases where one spouse files for divorce, drags the other through emotional hell, and then withdraws the petition, just to prolong the suffering. He was right.

The judge turned to my wife. "You have the right to withdraw your petition. However, I also have a counter-claim for divorce filed by your husband. Mr. Oglesby, do you wish to proceed?"

"Yes, Your Honor," I said. "I'd like to proceed with my counterclaim."

The judge looked back at my wife. "Would you like time to seek legal representation, or will you continue to represent yourself?"

"I'll represent myself," she replied.

The judge's tone grew firmer. "Mrs. Oglesby, I strongly recommend you seek legal counsel. There's a lot at stake, and this won't be easy."

"May I have a five-minute recess to think about it?" she asked.

The judge agreed. I knew exactly what that meant:

she was stepping out to call the "Man of God" for instructions.

When we returned, the judge asked for her decision. My wife said she would proceed on her own. She seemed emboldened, no doubt reassured by that phone call.

The judge then asked, "Who is your first witness?"

"My mother-in-law," she said.

My own mother took the stand. She testified that I was "fully retarded" and that this was the reason I left the cult. She claimed she feared I would sexually abuse my daughters now that I was no longer a member. Then she looked straight at me and told the judge that I was no longer her son, that I was dead to her.

The judge asked, "If he gains custody of your grandchildren, would you visit them?"

"No," my mother replied. "The only way I'll ever visit them is if he rejoins the House of Prayer."

The judge looked stunned. "I don't understand how you can say your son is mentally impaired when he's a certified HVAC technician who has supported his wife and twelve children, while she's never worked. That doesn't make sense."

It was clear to the judge—and to me—that this was part of the cult's campaign of demonization. I was astonished that my own mother would take part. But this was the price of loyalty to the "Man of God." To prove her allegiance, she had to publicly denounce her own son, the same son she once loved deeply.

It felt like being in a gang: blood in, blood out.

When my mother left the witness stand, the judge asked my wife, "Do you have another witness you'd like to call?"

"Yes, Your Honor," she said. "I'd like to call my husband to the stand."

I turned to my lawyer. "Is she allowed to call me as a witness?"

"Yes, she is," he replied. "You'll have to take the stand."

"Okay," I said. "If that's what she wants to do, then I'll do it."

I walked to the witness stand, was sworn in by the bailiff, and took my seat.

My wife looked directly at me. "The Bible says that you can only divorce your wife if she commits adultery. Is that true?"

"Yes," I replied calmly. "I'm aware of that."

With a condescending smirk, as if she had cornered me, she asked, "When did I commit adultery? Because if I haven't committed adultery, you cannot divorce me."

After a moment of thought, I responded, "You committed adultery when you filed for divorce from me, filed a restraining order based on lies, and had me thrown out of our home. You committed adultery when you refused to support me as I sought justice for the child molester who abused three of our kids."

"Objection, Your Honor!" she interrupted. "Can you please make him answer my questions?"

The judge looked at her firmly. "He is answering your question, ma'am. I told you that you needed representation, but you turned down my advice. It's not easy to question a witness. You may continue, Mr. Oglesby."

Before I spoke again, I glanced at the judge. She was leaning forward, listening intently, as if she truly wanted to hear the rest. So, I continued.

"You committed adultery when you taught our children to call me 'Pussy Lips.' You committed adultery when you had them call me 'Trashy-ass nigger.' You committed adultery when I tried to be intimate with you, and you opened the Bible to read scriptures while we were having sex. The 'Man of God' told you to do that, and you obeyed him, allowing another man to rob me of my affections with my wife. You committed adultery when you hid all my children from me and refused to allow any visitation."

That was my moment to tell the judge everything I had kept bottled up for so long. When I finished, my wife looked like she wished she had never asked me a single question. She turned to the judge and said quietly, "I have no further questions for him."

As I stepped down from the stand and returned to

my seat, my lawyer leaned toward me and whispered, "You did very well."

Next, the judge called the Guardian ad Litem to the stand and asked, "What were the results of your investigation?"

The Guardian ad Litem corroborated everything I had already told the court. She explained that in the so-called homeschool program established by the "Man of God," children ages twelve and thirteen were testing at a second- and third-grade level. She said the program was severely lacking and recommended that all the children be placed in public schools.

She went on to describe her conversation with the children's mother. She had asked her about the three children who were victims of the child molester—a member of the church—and whether she would be willing to keep them away from him. The mother refused to guarantee their safety. She even told the Guardian ad Litem that she disagreed with me for turning the molester in to the authorities, arguing that he was only a teenager when he committed the crimes, as if that somehow lessened the impact of what he did to our children.

The Guardian ad Litem then explained that she had also spoken with me. She visited my home and reported to the judge that I lived in a three-bedroom apartment, with separate, well-decorated rooms for the boys and girls—each furnished with bunk beds. She told the court that I had expressed my desire for my children to attend public school, go on to college, and live free from the cult's oppressive practices, such as arranged marriages at fourteen and being forced to have children without the option of birth control.

She also informed the judge that I had told her about my oldest son, who had recently left the "Man of God's" organization. She met with him as well. During their conversation, she asked him, "Who do you think should have custody of your brothers and sisters—your mother or your father?"

Without hesitation, my son answered, "My father should have custody."

Finally, the judge asked the Guardian ad Litem, "Based on your investigation, who do you believe would be in the best interest of the children to have custody?"

The Guardian ad Litem replied, "I believe the children should be given to their father."

After the Guardian ad Litem finished her testimony, the judge called for a thirty-minute recess before making her decision. When we returned to the courtroom, she announced that, due to the seriousness of the matter, she needed more time. She said she would mail her final decision within two weeks.

Final Order of Divorce

Two weeks later, the envelope arrived. I remember holding it in my hands, my heart pounding. I was nervous—almost afraid—to open it. The fact that the judge hadn't made an immediate ruling unsettled me. To me, it seemed so obvious that my children needed to be rescued from the grip and control of the "Man of God" and the congregation that my wife had willingly surrendered them to.

When I finally opened the letter, I saw that the judge had taken great care in writing her decision. The Final Order of Divorce was detailed and precise. These are the judge's words, exactly as they appeared:

Petitioner – Bronical Oglesby
Respondent – Michael Oglesby, Sr.

The parties were married on September 1, 1992, and separated in July 2011. Although this petition was originally filed by the Petitioner, at the start of the trial, the Petitioner withdrew her petition. The Respondent did not withdraw his counterclaim, so the trial proceeded on his counterclaim for divorce.

The Respondent has alleged this marriage to be irretrievably broken, and after having heard evidence on the matter, the Court finds it to be so.

It is the judgment of this Court that a total divorce be granted between the parties in the above-stated case, upon legal principles.

It is ordered by this Court that the marriage contract heretofore entered into between the parties to this case, from and after this date, be and is set aside and dissolved as fully and effectually as if no such contract had ever been made or entered into.

Petitioner and Respondent in the future shall be held and considered as separate and distinct persons altogether unconnected by any nuptial union or civil contract whatsoever, and both shall have the right to remarry.

Custody

The parties have twelve children, ten of whom are still unemancipated minors and subject to the provisions of this order. The minor children are Katrina, Maria, Nickolas, Cameron, Linda, Courtney, Patience, Shiphrah, Kiera, and Philip. (During the course of this trial, the Father made abundantly clear that he loves his two oldest children dearly and that they are always welcome in his home.)

Both parties were raised from young ages in the House of Prayer ("Church"). They were married when the Petitioner ("Mother") was fifteen and the Respondent ("Father") was eighteen years old.

Although he was extremely active in the Church, at some point the Father became disenchanted with it and decided to withdraw. The Father contends that when a member of the Church was alleged to have molested three of his children, along with other children in the congregation, the Church leadership discouraged the parties from contacting the proper authorities. They promised to handle the matter internally but failed to do so appropriately.

Although the Mother acknowledges that three of her children were victimized, she concurred with the Church's position that the alleged perpetrator should not have been reported to law enforcement. Her testimony at trial was deeply disturbing to the Court—she seemed to feel that the molester's age somehow lessened the severity of the crime, showing no recognition that the trauma inflicted upon the victims was equally devastating regardless of his age.

Apparently, the Church does not take kindly to "defections" such as the Father's. The Church initiated a campaign of ostracism against him. Unfortunately, both the Mother and the Father's own mother joined in this campaign.

As part of this effort—and perhaps out of her own resentment—the Mother consistently encouraged the children to ridicule and demean their father. She admitted in her testimony that she had gotten down on all fours in the presence of the children and the Father, barking like a dog and calling him one, while urging the children to do the same.

She also admitted to calling the Father vile names—

such as "nigger," "cocksucker," and "pussy licker"—in front of the children, encouraging them to repeat the words. When asked why she would behave this way in front of her 4-, 6-, 8-, and 9-year-old children, she testified that she did so "because it is true."

Since the parties' separation, she has withheld visitation from the Father and refused to cooperate in the criminal investigation of the man who molested her children.

The Father was a 38-year-old HVAC technician. Since the separation, he had continued—voluntarily—to pay the mortgage and utilities on the marital home. He had also taken steps to provide the children with a stable environment, securing a three-bedroom apartment furnished with bunk beds to accommodate them all. He felt that stepping away from the Church's influence had allowed him to reclaim his own life, and he described his efforts to take the children with him as an attempt to save theirs. He testified that the "home-schooling" required by the Church was inadequate.

He had compared his children's academic progress with that of children attending public schools and found the Church's version of "home-schooling" severely lacking. The Family Division Social Services Coordinator (Guardian Ad Lidem) recommended that custody be granted to the Father, in part due to the educational deficiencies she personally observed. She also noted that other families who had left the Church discovered, after enrolling their children in public schools, that the Church's "home-schooling" had left their children far behind.

The Court found the Father's actions—leaving the Church, reporting his children's abuser to legal authorities, standing firm against the Church's wrath and even his own family, and defending what he believed was right for himself and his children—to be noble and heroic acts of extraordinary courage. Even his own mother took the stand and testified that, because of his decision to leave both the Church and his family, she believed he was "all the way retarded."

There was also testimony that one of his two oldest children had sided with the Church and taken a firm stance against him. This was especially ironic, considering it was the Mother who had forced him out of the marital home and initiated the divorce proceedings.

For all these reasons, the Court found that it was in the best interest of the children for the Father to have sole legal and primary physical custody. The Father was granted full decision-making authority regarding all matters concerning the children—including education, religion, extracurricular activities, health, and mental well-being. The Mother was ordered to relinquish the children to the Father immediately.

VISITATION

The Mother may visit with the children at any time

agreed upon by both parties. In addition, she shall have the following visitation schedule:

For the months of February, March, and April 2013, the Mother may visit with the children on the third weekend of each month, beginning Friday at the close of school and ending Sunday at 6 p.m.

Beginning in May 2013, the Mother shall have visitation on the first and third weekends of each month, commencing Friday at the close of school (or 3 p.m. if there is no school) and continuing until Sunday at 6 p.m., allowing her the benefit of an extended weekend.

The Mother shall have the children with her on Mother's Day from 10 a.m. until 6 p.m., if Mother's Day falls during the Father's custodial time. The Father shall have the children with him on Father's Day from 10 a.m. until 6 p.m., if Father's Day falls during the Mother's custodial time.

The Mother shall have custody of the children for the first week of June and the first week of July each year.

For the Thanksgiving holiday, the Mother shall have the children during odd-numbered years, from 6 p.m. on the Sunday preceding Thanksgiving through the Sunday following Thanksgiving. The Father shall have the children for the Thanksgiving holiday during even-numbered years, regardless of whether it coincides with his regular visitation weekend.

For the Christmas holidays, the Father shall have the

children during the first period—from the day and time school is dismissed until December 26 at noon—in odd-numbered years. The Mother shall have the children from noon on December 26 until 6 p.m. on the day before school resumes. This winter vacation schedule shall alternate in even-numbered years.

In even-numbered years, the Mother shall have the right to visit with the children from 6 p.m. on the day they are dismissed from school for spring vacation until 6 p.m. on the Sunday immediately preceding the resumption of school. In odd-numbered years, the Father shall keep the children for the entire spring break.

Each party shall have the right to communicate with the children by telephone while they are in the other party's custody. Such communication shall be limited to one telephone call per day per child, unless otherwise agreed upon by both parties.

Neither party shall make disparaging remarks about the other in the presence of the children or to the children. Neither party shall film, record, or tape the other. Neither shall use the children to carry messages or money between them. Furthermore, neither party shall discuss this Order or its contents with the children, except when explaining visitation arrangements.

Marital Home and Alimony

The Mother is hereby awarded the parties' marital home in Atlanta. The Father shall continue to pay, as alimony, the mortgage, taxes, and insurance on said home through December 2015. During this period, the Mother shall make every effort to transfer the mortgage into her name.

In addition, as alimony, the Father shall pay the Mother's landline and cell phone bills (for any existing phones owned by the Mother), as well as her gas, sewer, water, and electric bills, her car note, and her car insurance. Beginning June 1, 2013, she shall assume responsibility for her car insurance and car note, if any, and the Father shall no longer be responsible for them.

Child Support

The Mother has been essentially unemployed throughout the marriage. She obtained her GED this past year. The Court suspends child support temporarily to allow the Mother time to gain skills and secure employment. Beginning January 1, 2014, the Mother shall pay child support in the amount of $650.00 per month.

Child support shall continue monthly until each child reaches the age of eighteen, dies, marries, or otherwise becomes emancipated. However, if a child reaches eighteen while enrolled in and attending secondary school full-time, support shall continue until the child graduates or reaches twenty years of age, whichever occurs first.

Nothing in this Order precludes the parties from reaching an agreement to offset child support and alimony payments when the periods for them overlap.

Automobiles

The Father shall retain the parties' sixteen-passenger van and all vehicles connected to his electrical and HVAC business. The Mother shall retain the parties' Lincoln automobile. Each party shall execute any and all documents necessary to transfer title of said vehicles to the other.

As of September 1, 2013, each party shall be solely responsible for all insurance, payments, liabilities, taxes, repairs, and upkeep of the vehicles they have retained under this Order.

SO ORDERED, this 23rd day of January, 2013.

The Order and the Illusion of Peace

When the Final Divorce Order arrived in the mail, I held it in my hands like a trophy. Ten pages long—unusually detailed, almost poetic in its precision. The judge had written with care, outlining not just her ruling but the reasoning behind every decision. It was as if she wanted to leave no room for misinterpretation, no space for revisionist history.

She had ruled in my favor, yet she had shown compassion toward my ex-wife. That balance, that nuance, made the document feel more than legal—it felt prophetic.

I remember thinking, This is it. The war is over. I had

fought for my children and won. I had stood alone against a system that didn't always listen to fathers, and I had prevailed. That decree was supposed to mark the end of the nightmare.

But it wasn't.

The "Man of God"—the one who had orchestrated so much pain behind the scenes—wasn't finished. His influence didn't stop at the courthouse steps. It seeped into my home like smoke under a door. Even with custody, even with the law on my side, I wasn't truly free. My children had been shaped by years of indoctrination, and his reach extended through whispers, phone calls, and spiritual manipulation.

That's when I began to realize that winning custody was only the beginning. The real battle wasn't fought in a courtroom—it was for their hearts, their minds, their sense of safety. And I wasn't just fighting a man. I was fighting a belief system, a shadow network of control that didn't respect boundaries or court orders.

Maybe the judge knew. Maybe that's why she wrote so carefully, so thoroughly. Maybe she saw what I couldn't yet see—that I would need this decree not just as proof of victory, but as armor for the war that was still to come.

I asked my cousin to give me a ride to my children's home so I could pick them up and retrieve the sixteen-passenger van that the Court had awarded me to transport them. I was granted custody of ten of my twelve children, since my two oldest sons were at least eighteen and legally emancipated at that time.

When I arrived at my ex-wife's house, I went to the door expecting some resistance from the kids. Surprisingly, they came out of the house peacefully—except for my two oldest daughters. They lingered in the living room with their mother, hesitating to leave. I walked inside to encourage them to come on out and get in the van. As they were walking toward the door, I overheard them tell their mother, "Don't worry about nothing, Momma, because we got your back."

A surge of fear shot up my spine. In that instant, I understood that a plot was unfolding—one orchestrated by the "Man of God" and my ex-wife, using my children as pawns to rebel against me. Oprah Winfrey often talks about having "Ah-hah" moments. Well, that day, I didn't have an "Ah-hah" moment—if memory serves me right, I had more of an "Ah, shit" moment.

I had seen the "Man of God" manipulate people and twist situations against anyone he considered an enemy. I knew how cunning he could be. The fear I felt wasn't paranoia—it was a justified fear, built from years of watching him operate. He had the spirit of a sly fox and knew exactly how to use and manipulate people.

I could tell my children were happy to come with me, to leave behind the rigid life of the cult. But at the same time, they felt a deep loyalty to their mother—a loyalty the "Man of God" knew how to exploit to his advantage. I realized I was engaged in a real-life chess match with a master player, and honestly, I didn't feel capable of defeating him on my own. My only hope was to rely on help from God through Christ Jesus, the one in whom I placed my faith.

At the time, I was renting a three-bedroom apartment in anticipation of gaining custody of my kids. It was small, especially for eleven people, but I had each room carefully decorated with enough bunk beds to make space for all of them.

CHAPTER 23
KNOWING THE PLAYBOOK

WHEN SURVIVAL BECOMES STRATEGY

I didn't just survive the "Man of God." I learned his playbook.

I knew the tactics, the timing, the tone. I knew when he was about to shift blame, when he was about to twist scripture, when he was about to turn a rebuke into a performance. I had seen it all—up close, for years.

That's what made my survival different. I wasn't just running from abuse. I was running with knowledge.

I understood how he manipulated emotions: how he used fear to control, shame to silence, and charisma to confuse. I knew how he weaponized scripture—not to heal, but to dominate. I saw how he built loyalty through isolation and how obedience became identity.

Because I knew the playbook, I could spot the

patterns. Not just in him, but in others like him. In churches. In relationships. In systems.

Knowing the playbook meant I could help others escape. I could say, "This isn't just wrong—it's rehearsed." I could say, "You're not crazy. You're being played."

It also meant I had to unlearn a lot. When you've memorized the playbook, it lives in you. It shapes your reactions, your relationships, your theology. Healing meant rewriting every page.

But I did it. And I'm still doing it.

Because surviving the "Man of God" wasn't just about leaving the building. It was about reclaiming my mind, my faith, and my voice.

CHAPTER 24
RECLAIMING MY HOME

THE QUIET INVASION

Even after the judge's gavel fell and the decree was signed, peace didn't follow. The "Man of God" had lost in court, but not in spirit. His influence lingered like smoke—unseen but suffocating. My children, though physically safe, were still tethered to his teachings, his voice, his control.

I had won custody, but I hadn't yet won freedom.

CHAPTER 25
THE FIRE AND THE PEACE

For nearly two years, my life had been a battlefield—emotionally, spiritually, and legally. Every step toward reclaiming my children felt like a fight against an invisible force determined to keep us apart.

Even after the courtroom testimonies, the Guardian ad Litem's support, and the truth finally being spoken aloud, there was still interference. The "Man of God" continued to insert himself into our lives—manipulating, controlling, and sowing division between my children and me. Peace always felt just out of reach.

For more than six months after gaining custody, I was still fighting his long reach from the pulpit into my home.

But then, everything changed.

The Fire That Spoke

The man who had orchestrated so much pain and confusion—who built an empire of fear cloaked in scripture—died suddenly in a house fire. The news was surreal.

For years, he had loomed over our lives like a shadow, interfering with my children's healing, poisoning their minds, and keeping our family fractured. But in the silence that followed his death, something shifted. The tension that had gripped us began to loosen. The spiritual fog that clouded my children's hearts started to lift.

For the first time in years, we could breathe.

It wasn't just the absence of his voice—it was the absence of his control. And in that void, peace began to bloom.

What struck me most was the symbolism of his death. Fire had followed him for years, like a divine warning he refused to heed. The first church building he led burned to the ground—no lives lost, but the structure was completely consumed. Then there was the van—he and his closest friend were driving when it suddenly burst into flames. They barely escaped. Another time, while using torches to strip paint from a house, the entire structure ignited. And once more, his own home caught fire while he was away, badly damaged but not destroyed.

Each time, fire came close. Each time, he walked away. It was as if God had been whispering through the flames, offering him a chance to turn back, to repent, to release the grip he held over so many lives.

And then, the final fire came—and this time, he did not escape.

To some, it may have seemed like a coincidence. But to me, it felt like divine punctuation. A series of warnings ignored. A reckoning fulfilled. The man who had preached control and twisted scripture for his own gain was consumed by the very element that had shadowed him for years.

His death didn't erase the trauma, but it marked the beginning of restoration. My children began to laugh again. They started to ask questions. They began to see me—not as the villain they'd been taught to fear—but as the father who had never stopped fighting for them.

The fire that took his life didn't just end his chapter —it ignited ours.

It wasn't only the absence of his influence—it was the presence of something new: peace, clarity, and healing. My children began to open up. They laughed more. They asked questions. They started to see me, truly see me. We began to bond in ways that once seemed impossible.

Meals together. Conversations without fear. Even silence felt sacred, because it wasn't filled with dread.

I realized then that this wasn't just the end of a chapter—it was the beginning of restoration. The fire that took his life marked the end of an era of oppression, but it also sparked something new in ours: freedom.

And with that freedom came responsibility. I knew I had to continue guiding my children—not just away from the cult, but toward a life of purpose, education, and self-worth. I had to show them what love looked like without manipulation. What faith felt like without fear. What family meant when it was built on truth.

The road ahead wouldn't be easy. Trauma doesn't vanish overnight. But for the first time, we were walking it together.

It started subtly. My children would quote him in conversation. They'd speak of obedience, of spiritual warfare, of loyalty to a man who had never truly protected them. I saw fear in their eyes when I challenged those ideas, and confusion when I tried to offer love without strings.

They had been conditioned to believe that love was something earned through submission, not something freely given.

The Resistance Within

I realized I wasn't just rebuilding a family, I was deprogramming trauma. I had to become both father and healer. I had to create a home that felt safe, physically, emotionally, and spiritually.

That meant long talks at bedtime. It meant listening more than lecturing. It meant showing them, day by day, that love doesn't manipulate—it liberates.

There were setbacks. There were moments when I questioned whether I was strong enough. But I kept going. I kept praying. I kept showing up.

I surrounded my children with truth, with kindness, with consistency. I let them see me cry. I let them see me laugh. I let them see me as a man—not a prophet, not a tyrant, just a father who refused to give up.

The Shift

Slowly, the fog began to lift. My children started asking questions. They began challenging the teachings they once accepted without thought.

They started to trust me—not just as a provider, but as a protector. The "Man of God" lost his grip, not because I fought him directly, but because I gave my children something stronger to hold onto: love without fear.

Closing Reflection

Reclaiming my home wasn't about tearing down walls; it was about building new ones. It was about creating a space where truth could breathe, where laughter could echo, and where healing could begin.

The court gave me custody, but it was love that gave me my children back.

CHAPTER 26
FROM SURVIVAL TO STRENGTH

The First Signs of Light

It didn't happen overnight. Healing rarely does.

But one day, I noticed my daughter humming a song that wasn't from the House of Prayer. It was just a pop tune on the radio, but to me, it felt like a breakthrough.

My son started asking questions—real questions—about the world, about God, about choice. They were beginning to think for themselves. That was the first sign that the fog was lifting.

I didn't push. I didn't preach. I just stayed present.

I made pancakes on Saturdays. I let them sleep in. I gave them space to be kids again. Slowly, laughter returned to our home—not the forced kind, not the kind that hides pain, but the kind that bubbles up from joy.

Building a New Foundation

I knew I couldn't erase the past, but I could build something new.

I enrolled them in counseling. I found mentors who spoke truth with love. I surrounded them with people who didn't want to control them, just support them. And I kept showing up. Every school event. Every late-night talk. Every moment they needed me, I was there.

We started new traditions: movie nights, game nights, Sunday dinners with no sermons, just stories.

I let them decorate their rooms however they wanted. I let them choose. That was the key: giving them back their power.

Finding My Own Strength

In the process of helping them heal, I found healing too.

I stopped blaming myself. I stopped replaying the past. I started writing, praying, breathing. I found peace in the small things—in the way my son hugged me without hesitation, in the way my daughter said "I love you" without fear.

I realized that strength isn't about winning battles, it's about enduring them. It's about staying soft in a world that tries to harden you. It's about choosing love, again and again, even when it's hard.

Closing Reflection

We're not perfect. We're not finished. But we're free.

And that freedom is sacred. It was earned through tears, through truth, through relentless love.

The "Man of God" may have tried to break us, but he failed—because love, real love, doesn't bow to fear.

This chapter of our lives is no longer about survival. It's about strength. It's about joy. It's about reclaiming everything we were told we couldn't have.

And we're just getting started.

CHAPTER 27
THRIVING IN THE LIGHT

New Roots, New Growth

Once the dust settled and the shadows receded, something remarkable began to happen: my children started to thrive. Not just survive, but truly live. The trauma didn't vanish overnight, but healing became visible—in their laughter, in their curiosity, and in the way they began to dream again.

My daughter, once withdrawn and cautious, started singing and writing songs. Her lyrics were raw, beautiful, and brave—each line a step away from fear and toward freedom. Watching her find her voice was like watching sunlight break through clouds that had hung for too long.

I watched all my children bloom, and I knew deep down: this was the fruit of the fight.

Education and Empowerment

Academically, they soared. Freed from the mental weight of manipulation, they began to excel. Teachers noticed. Counselors noticed. Their confidence grew, and with it, their curiosity. They weren't just catching up—they were leaping forward.

We talked about college, about careers, about purpose. I encouraged them to explore, to question, and to build their own beliefs. I didn't want to shape their minds; I wanted to protect their freedom to shape their own.

Each new conversation reminded me how powerful freedom truly is. What once felt impossible was becoming their everyday reality.

Faith Reimagined

Spiritually, we found a new rhythm. We didn't abandon faith—we reclaimed it. We prayed together, not out of obligation, but out of gratitude.

We talked about God, not as a weapon, but as a source of love and justice. I let them ask hard questions.

I let them wrestle with doubt. And in that space of honesty and grace, they found something real.

Faith, I learned, is not about control. It's about connection. It's about finding light in places you were once told to fear.

Giving Back

As we healed, I felt a calling to share our story. I began speaking to other parents—those still in the fight, still trapped in the fog. I told them what I had learned: that love is louder than control, that truth is stronger than fear, and that no battle is ever truly lost if you keep showing up.

I started writing. I started mentoring. I became a voice for those who felt voiceless. And in doing so, I found purpose beyond pain.

Giving back wasn't just about helping others—it was part of my own healing. Every time I spoke, I felt another layer of weight lift from my spirit.

Closing Reflection

This chapter isn't just about my children—it's about legacy. It's about turning wounds into wisdom. It's about proving that even the deepest scars can become symbols of survival.

We are thriving. Not because the road was easy, but because we refused to stop walking it. Every step forward is a testament to the power of truth, the strength of love, and the resilience of family.

The light we live in now isn't borrowed—it's our own.

PART V
LEGACY AND LETTERS

CHAPTER 28
LETTERS FROM MY CHILDREN

A Letter from My Oldest Daughter, Katrina

Dear Dad,

I had no idea who I was until you rescued me. I didn't know the power I had within. If you hadn't saved me, I don't know if I would've ever had the opportunity to pursue my journey of self-discovery, purpose, and self-love.

Because of you, I am free to live, love, laugh, and learn without limits. You gave me the space to decide what Katrina wants—and who Katrina wants to be. You showed me selfless love and true altruism. You sacrificed everything for me.

I am courageous, brave, and strong because of you and the strength you've passed on to me. God blessed me with that same determination, and I'm so grateful, especially in a world that can be tough to grow up and find your way in. But through it all, I'm so thankful to have you by my side and in my corner, always. I love you so much.

With your help, I discovered what I'm truly passionate about—people, and improving humanity one person at a time. I'm grateful to you because, throughout this journey, you've given me every resource to pursue my passion fully and with unwavering support. For that, I will forever be thankful.

I now hold a B.A. in Biology from Kennesaw State University, and I'm attending medical school at Southern Illinois University. My cup truly runneth over with blessings. You positioned me for success, and God did the rest.

Sometimes I feel so blessed and highly favored that I can't even explain how things work out the way they do. But we both know—it's God and His favor upon our lives. His plan always surpasses our own. God just wants us to get in position so He can move in our lives and help manifest our prayers and desires into reality. He blessed us for stepping out in faith and trusting in His promise to make a way out of no way.

God has kept His promise to me. He's ensured my safety and success so far, and I will continue to count on Him.

God truly used you as the catalyst that prepared me—and all of us—for Him to move on our behalf and perform miracle after miracle in our lives. I know I am a walking testimony, a miracle in human form. Stereotypes and statistics do not define me. I am an outlier—a warrior here for a higher purpose. You and I both are.

One thing I know for sure is that you prepared us for this moment. You raised us to believe in ourselves and to trust our intuition when solving problems. One of the things I've always loved about you is your emphasis on education, logical thinking, and common sense. You've never underestimated the power of knowledge or the importance of being informed.

I've always known you were a sharp thinker—deeply intelligent—and I've admired that about you all my life.

Growing up, you made sure our activities challenged us mentally. You surrounded us with educational games and activities that focused on memory, vocabulary, speed, and skill. You filled our shelves with books, puzzles, and word games that sharpened our minds. You also encouraged our singing and piano lessons, helping me embrace my creativity and personality.

I can truly say, "Daddy didn't raise no fool!"

You're an incredible piano player, and I've always loved our family time together. You make life fun, full of laughter, and free.

Because of you, I know my self-worth. My self-esteem isn't tied only to my achievements, but to the person I am within. I am proud of who I've become—and even prouder to be your daughter.

I'm so happy you're my daddy, and that I am your oldest girl. I wouldn't want it any other way.

With all my love,

Katrina

Letter from Maria Oglesby

How Did My Dad Leaving the House of Prayer Affect Me?

When I was in the House of Prayer, I was not happy. The lifestyle that my family and the members of the congregation lived was very robotic. Every person was discouraged from having free will or independent thought.

The unspoken rule for staying in good standing was simple: never challenge the majority, never disobey the pastor—whether you agreed with him or not—and never socialize with anyone who was not a member of the organization.

As you can imagine, this way of thinking caused many families to be torn apart, including my own.

At that time, I had no real goals in life. I was expected to follow the traditions of the congregation: get married in my early teens, have many children, and settle into a life without any other aspirations. I had no opportunity to express my feelings in that environment. I had few friends within the community, and certainly none outside of it. Most of the time, I felt alone.

To make matters worse, the pastor didn't like me. That alone made me an outsider early in my childhood. I was constantly under scrutiny. There were times I was rebuked in front of the entire congregation for no reason at all. I used to wish one of my parents would leave, but I thought they were too devoted to ever make that decision.

When my dad finally left, I was still carrying the trauma of being excluded and rejected by the members. Even after he left, my siblings and I still wanted to be part of his life, so we continued to spend time with him despite his decision to leave the church.

When my mom told the leader that we were still seeing our dad, he became furious. He instructed everyone in the church not to speak to us until he said otherwise—and everyone obeyed.

During that time, I went through a lot of emotional trauma, much of which lingered even after I was physically out of that environment. The first two years outside the House of Prayer were the hardest for me. After spending more than half my life under those conditions, I felt like I still had to follow certain traditions, like wearing long dresses. But once I overcame that mindset, my worldview began to expand.

Ever since my dad made the decision to get my siblings and me out of that place, I've accomplished so much—and I intend to accomplish even more.

One of the first positive changes I noticed after leaving was how much more academically challenged I became. In the homeschool run by members of the congregation, our education was limited. The main goal of that homeschool was to reduce contact with anyone outside the House of Prayer.

While I have nothing against homeschooling itself, the problem was that the women who ran it were not licensed teachers and, at most, had only a high school education. As a result, what we learned depended entirely on their limited knowledge.

When I entered public high school at age fifteen, I felt challenged academically for the first time. My mind began to open. That's also where I was introduced to Spanish—and I fell in love with the language. Over time, I learned enough to speak and understand it at an intermediate level. I know that if I had remained in that environment, I never would have reached my academic potential.

In 2016, I was accepted into Valdosta State University. That moment was incredibly exciting because not many people in my family had ever gone to or graduated from college. I chose to attend because I wanted to explore a new environment beyond my hometown, even though I was heavily discouraged by family members who were still part of the organization.

That same year, I had the privilege of traveling to Washington, D.C., where I shadowed the late and honorable Congressman John Lewis.

In 2019, I earned a $10,000 scholarship to study abroad in London, England. Traveling abroad broadened my perspective on people and cultures. In the House of Prayer, I had been taught that anyone who didn't live by the congregation's rules was a bad person. But my study abroad experience taught me something very different: just because people live differently doesn't make them wrong.

It was an experience I will never forget, and I know it wouldn't have been possible if I were still living under that strict system. If I had stayed, I likely would have been punished for even thinking about traveling or exploring the world.

In 2020, I graduated from Valdosta State University with a B.A. in Psychology. Not only did I graduate, but I did so with honors—**Magna Cum Laude**, with a 3.8 GPA.

Now, I plan to attend graduate school abroad in Spain, majoring in Public Health with a minor in Spanish.

By the end of this letter, I hope you can see the profound, positive shift that has taken place in my life since my dad made that bold, life-changing decision. Because of him, I now live the life God intended for me to its fullest.

Today, I am able to make my own decisions about my future without fear of being criticized or punished. When I was in that environment, it felt like my life story had already been written for me. My sense of self—and my right to choose—were stripped away from the moment I was born.

But when my dad made the courageous choice to remove me from those harsh conditions, it was like he handed me the pen so I could finally write my own story—and decide how it ends.

A Letter from Nickolas Oglesby

I strongly believe my father made the right decision when he took my siblings and me out of the church we were part of. It's not as simple as saying they were wrong and my dad was right, nor do I hold much hostility toward the church. If I'm being honest, I believe they were right about a lot of things. It was their execution of those beliefs that left me questioning what I was being taught during my time there. And yes, I'll also admit that the church did things I completely disagreed with.

Still, I don't think it's fair to judge them solely by their wrongdoings. They are, despite their flaws, human at the end of the day. They also did many good things for people on various occasions. But the primary reason I believe it was best for us to leave is that my potential was being greatly wasted there.

I take deep pride in saying that my father is the greatest man I know. I've always looked up to him with the highest respect and admiration. I'll never forget the trials he endured to get us out of that church. Some of those trials still weigh on my conscience, and probably always will.

If I'm being truthful, I never intended to speak publicly about what happened. But I've realized it's only fair to him to tell the truth. His name was dragged through the mud on live television by that church. They said he abandoned his wife and kids — a heartless lie that will never be anything more than that. Michael Oglesby never abandoned his children. He has been there from the moment each of us was born and remains present in our lives today.

That lie came from the church's leader, who did everything in his power to hurt my father for leaving. I was too afraid to stand up to him, too afraid to challenge his authority — and so were most of the members. I know that by saying this, the church may no longer want anything to do with me. But deep down, they know I'm telling the truth.

One of my favorite book series of all time is Harry Potter by J.K. Rowling. I often think of a quote from one of my favorite characters, Albus Dumbledore: "There will come a time when you must choose between what is easy and what is right."

It would be easy for me to pretend everything is fine, to act as though I agree with how they tried to discredit and destroy my father. But the right thing to do is to speak the truth — to admit that their actions caused great damage to our family, even if that means they never speak to me again.

I must stop being afraid to speak my mind. When the time comes to stand up for what is right, I want to be remembered as someone who always did exactly that.

The truth is, my potential was being wasted in that

church. My father has always believed in education and wanted his children to be intelligent and self-sufficient. That's why he never catered to us too much. He pushed us to go to school, learn what we could, and apply that knowledge to the real world. It wasn't just about showing up, doing homework, and getting good grades. He wanted to know how we were using what we learned to better ourselves.

I still remember one day when my father was cutting my hair. I must have been about eight years old and still in that church. Out of nowhere, he asked what kind of work I wanted to do when I grew up. It caught me completely off guard because I was used to him cutting my hair in silence.

I quickly said I might work at McDonald's or become a landscaper. He asked if there was anything else I wanted to do, but I had no answer. Then he told me I should look beyond the walls that surrounded me — to see if I was capable of more.

At the time, I didn't understand. I didn't see why it mattered where I worked as long as I had a job. But now I understand what he was trying to uncover with that question. Back then, I was simply reflecting what I saw around me. Most of the church members worked in landscaping or fast food. There were exceptions, but that seemed to be the pattern.

Those who had other skills used them well, but the

younger generation wasn't being taught how to acquire or improve such skills. If I had stayed, I fear I'd still be trying to figure out how to make a living. My father saw that too — that's why he asked me that question.

While in the church, I was homeschooled and told that all I needed was a GED. They believed children shouldn't attend public schools because of restrictions on public prayer. Many members felt that without prayer, God was no longer present in public schools, leaving them unprotected and overly focused on education instead of faith.

I understand where they were coming from. People should have the right to pray if that's their belief. But I don't think the church handled this issue properly. Because we lacked the funding of public schools, our resources were extremely limited, and we could only learn so much.

I hold no resentment toward the teachers in the church's homeschooling program. I know they truly tried their best. It just wasn't enough for me to develop properly. That's why I say my potential was being wasted. I've always had a deep desire to learn and a mind eager to grow.

I've heard that their educational system has since improved, and I sincerely hope that's true. I just want people to understand why it didn't work for me back then.

When my father gained full custody, and I entered public school for the first time, I realized how far behind I was. I attended Lindley Middle School for my eighth-grade year in 2013–2014. At first, I was afraid and unsure of myself. I've always struggled with anxiety, and during that time, it was at an all-time high.

I actually had several panic attacks during my first year of public school, though I didn't know what they were or how to talk about them. It was one of the lowest points in my life. I felt fragile and vulnerable in an unfamiliar world.

But after about four months, I not only caught up, I found myself slightly ahead of most of my peers. I'm far from a genius, but I've always valued knowledge. I knew I had to work harder than everyone else because they'd had such a head start.

I'll never forget the teachers who helped me through that year. Mrs. Johnson, Mrs. Varney, Mrs. Webb, and Ms. Jones — I'll always remember you. If you ever happen to read this, thank you for everything.

I'm still maturing today, and I feel like my journey is only beginning. But when I look back, I see how far I've come. I attended and graduated from New Manchester High School and went on to pursue a career in welding.

I don't say any of this to hurt anyone. I still visit the church sometimes because I truly hold no hatred toward them. I love everyone there and hope they don't feel hostility toward me after reading this. But if they do, I'll accept it, because I believe I'm doing the right thing — and I'm being honest about how I feel.

Honesty was, after all, something that the church valued deeply.

My mother is still a member, and I love her as much as ever. I know she may not like some of the things I've said, but I hold nothing against her. She sacrificed so much for me — a debt I can never fully repay.

My older brother, Matthew, is also still a member, along with his wife and three kids. And to this day, Matthew is my favorite brother. I don't care what church he attends; I'll love him no differently. We still talk almost every week, just like we always have. We've always gotten along because we have so much in common, and I hope nothing changes that.

And to my father — thank you for everything you've ever done for me. I can't even find the words to express how much I appreciate you. I'll always remember this incredibly difficult journey. It has made us all so much stronger.

A Letter from Linda Oglesby

The irony of my passion for the performing arts still pierces me. It requires freedom, vulnerability, stamina, agility, tenacity, and fitness — all of which were discouraged in the House of Prayer cult. The very act of dancing or singing anything other than old hymns would earn me a whipping. Questioning any belief of the cult was met with swift correction. My curiosity was quickly silenced.

The truth is, if Daddy had never listened to that small voice in his head urging him to leave, I would have turned eighteen still brainwashed, married young, likely with a couple of kids, overweight, and spiritually disturbed. I would never have breathed life into my artistry or into my God-given talents and abilities. I would have remained ignorant of my own identity, never shaking hands with the essence of who I am. Ironically, I would have never known who God truly is or the power He holds.

Academically, I would have been lost as well; my performance was nothing short of pitiful. Surely, I wouldn't have graduated high school with a 3.8 GPA, ranking in the top ten percent of my class while taking mostly AP and Honors courses, the most rigorous of them all.

So, to my dad, I say thank you — for quite frankly

saving my life. For giving me the simple but profound gift of choice: the option to live or not. For challenging me to define what living even means. And for being my first introduction to real love. You are stoic and resilient, and you deserve nothing less than rich peace, rich health, rich love, and abundance–nothing to the contrary.

CHAPTER 29
KEEP IT MOVING

There are times when I'm tempted to feel sorry for myself for the trauma I endured at the hands of the "Man of God." But I'm quickly reminded of how short life is — and how there's no time for anger, unforgiveness, or self-pity, especially when others still rely on me for strength and stability along life's journey.

You can't lead a family while drowning in self-pity. Life is about what's next. No matter the defeats or traumas you experience, you must stay focused on what lies ahead.

I once had a friend I met in HVAC school who, along with his family, took me in after I made my exodus from the Man of God's church. They extended their arms of friendship at a time when I desperately needed it. I'll always remember the kindness his mother, sisters, and grandparents showed me during one of the most vulnerable seasons of my life.

Back then, I walked around soaked in anger, regret, and self-pity. Every time I spoke with my friend's grandfather, I found myself reliving the pain of my past, telling stories of my sad upbringing — usually followed by bitter tears and an unspoken hope for sympathy. At first, Granddad would listen patiently, offering words of comfort. But after a while, his response changed.

He began to speak with the calm wisdom that nearly ninety years of living had taught him. His decades of experience distilled into a simple three-word phrase: **"Keep it moving."**

Whenever I started my sympathetic tirade, Granddad would look at me and say, "Mike, you must keep it moving. And in all things, give thanks. Everything you're going through—not only did God allow it, but He chose it for you. God is about to push you into your destiny. He's reshaping your character, moving you from faith to favor. He's taking you out of your comfort zone, teaching you to trust Him more, and helping you become self-reliant. You should even thank those who hurt and betrayed you, because they helped set you free."

At the time, I didn't fully understand what he meant. But looking back now, I see the truth in his words. I learned things I never could have learned any other way.

I met people I never would have met otherwise. I discovered that I had more strength than I ever imagined.

I thought I would lose my mind going through it all —but instead, I realized how tough I really was. When I look at my children today, I see the opportunities they now have — opportunities they might never have known if we hadn't endured those hardships.

I've learned to thank God not only for the good things in life, but also for the bad and the ugly. Because the scripture says, "All things work together for good to them who love God and are called according to His purpose."

When my wife filed for divorce and a restraining order against me — both on the same day — I didn't realize it at the time, but she was giving me a gift. I was like a slave who had just received his freedom papers, though I didn't yet understand it. She did me a favor without knowing it.

There was so much I needed to learn — about myself, about people, about life. I had to go through what I went through. I didn't know how I was going to "keep it moving," but I knew I had to. I couldn't stay bogged down in that pit of anger and self-pity any longer.

Once I accepted that truth, God began to give me a plan — a way forward. It started with rescuing my children from that cult led by the "Man of God," which was nothing more than a graveyard for dreams.

If you dreamed of becoming a doctor, that dream would die there.

If you wanted to be a teacher, it would die there.

If you hoped to be a lawyer, it would die there.

If my daughters dreamed of becoming President or Vice President of the United States, that dream, too, would die in that place.

I knew I had a responsibility — to make sure my children were placed in an environment where their dreams and aspirations could not only survive, but thrive. They deserved access to the opportunities that life offers to anyone willing to work for them.

The Victory

After months of hearings, investigations, and mediation, the court made its decision: **I was awarded full custody of my children.**

It wasn't just a legal victory—it was a spiritual one. It was proof that truth, when spoken with courage, can pierce through the noise. It was proof that a father's love, when rooted in faith, can overcome even the most powerful opposition.

My children came home. And while the road ahead was still long, it was ours to walk together.

Closing Reflection

I didn't win custody because I was perfect. I won because I refused to give up—because I chose to speak truth in a system that often silences fathers. I believed that God would make a way, and He did.

This chapter of my life taught me that real strength isn't loud. It's steady. It's faithful. It's the kind of strength that shows up every day, even when no one's watching.

And now, every time I see my children laugh, learn, and grow, I know the fight was worth it.

Lessons Moving Forward

1. **Mending relationships** I had once given up on.
2. **Reclaiming my ambitions** and rediscovering my talents after years of denying them for the sake of the "man of God."
3. **Recognizing false love**—the conditional affection that once felt like acceptance but was merely control disguised as care.

Each of these lessons became a part of my healing. They helped me rebuild not only my life but also my identity.

For years, I lived under their rules, their control,

their version of reality. But now, I write my own story. The scars remain, but they are proof that I survived—that I escaped, that I am free.

I am not the person they told me I had to be.

I am who I choose to become.

And that is a kind of freedom they will never understand.

Printed in Great Britain
by Amazon

403cbfc3-5521-4172-b6e0-aeb4192a7eaeR01